Alexander Hamilton Bullock

A commemorative Address at Royalston. August 23rd, 1865

The hundredth Anniversary of its Incorporation

Alexander Hamilton Bullock

A commemorative Address at Royalston. August 23rd, 1865
The hundredth Anniversary of its Incorporation

ISBN/EAN: 9783337080198

Printed in Europe, USA, Canada, Australia, Japan

Cover: Foto ©ninafisch / pixelio.de

More available books at **www.hansebooks.com**

COMMEMORATIVE ADDRESS,

AT ROYALSON, AUGUST 23d, 1865;

The Hundredth Anniversary of its Incorporation.

BY

Hon. A. H. Bullock,

OF WORCESTER.

WITH THE

POEM, OTHER PROCEEDINGS,

AND

AN APPENDIX.

WINCHENDON:
PRINTED BY FRANK W. WARD.
1865.

Commonwealth of Massachusetts.

Executive Department,

Boston, April 9th 1866

Commonwealth of Massachusetts.

Executive Department.

Boston, April 9th 1866

PREFACE.

The object of this volume is to present and transmit the accomplished history of Royalston's First Century.

In pursuance of this object prominence has been given to the able and comprehensive Commemoration Address of the Hon. ALEXANDER H. BULLOCK, delivered at the recent Centennial of the Town.

Appended thereto will be found a series of notes, covering materials deemed worthy of preservation, as either illustrating the text and contributing to the fullness of the history therein out-lined, or valuable for future reference. For these materials, obligation is due in great part to the contributions of Benoni Peck, Esq., of Fitzwilliam,—a native, and, till lately, an honored citizen of Royalston, and his son, Henry Peck, of Winchendon, and to the labors of the Historical Committee, whose preparation for our late celebration was both laborious and effective.

It was manifestly proper, as certainly it was expected, that some connected report of the Centennial should be given in these pages. By general consent it was a success. Its records here will be grateful to those who participated in it, interesting to friends prevented from doing so, and it may indicate, to those who shall celebrate the Bi-Centennial of Royalston, how these things were done in the dim and distant past.

Anxious to bring this volume within modest limits, and to delay as little as possible its issue, we may have failed in fullness of selection, and extent of original investigation. We have aimed, however, to be just to historical facts, and impartial toward the various sections and interests of the town.

Hoping that the next contribution to the history of Royalston may be drawn from more copious sources, through the more abundant prosperity of the town, and that its execution may fall into abler hands, this memorial volume is commended to the considerate reception of the citizens, natives, descendants and friends of the town.

      E. W. BULLARD, } Committee
      DANIEL DAVIS,   } of
      JOSEPH R. EATON. } Publication.

ROYALSTON, September, 1865.

REPORT

OF THE

ROYALSTON CENTENNIAL.

The question of celebrating the Hundredth anniversary of the settlement and incorporation of Royalston, had frequently been discussed, but no public action was taken thereon till April 4th, 1864, when the Town chose a committee of seven to consider and report upon that question.

The committee, consisting of Rev. E. W. Bullard, S. S. Farrar, Jarvis Davis, Esq., J. L. Perkins, Cyrus Davis, John N. Bartlett, and Luther Harrington, reported to the Town Nov. 8th, 1864, the following recommendations:

"1. That Wednesday, Aug. 23d, 1865, be the day for observing the commemorative services of the settlement and incorporation of the good old town of Royalston, now on the eve of its hundredth anniversary.

2. That these services be, a Commemorative Address, Poems, a free collation, with appropriate religious exercises.

3. That Royalston's honored son, and Massachusett's peerless orator, the Hon. Alexander H. Bullock, be invited to deliver the Address, and Samuel C. Gale, Esq., and Albert Bryant, A. M., the Poems.

4. That a committee of —— citizens of Royalston be chosen by the town to invite the aforesaid gentlemen to perform for us these labors of love, and to arrange for and carry out to their consummation, in a liberal and earnest spirit, worthy of the town, the foregoing recommendations.

5. That the Town choose a committee of seven to make researches in reference to the history of Royalston, with a view to their preservation and ultimate publication, if it should be deemed advisable.

6. That the Town, for the purposes aforesaid, raise and appropriate the sum of —— dollars."

Recommendations 1, 2, and 3, were adopted by the town; the blank in 4 was filled by *fifteen*, a committee of six, consisting of Joseph Raymond, Esq., Edmund Stockwell, Geo. Whitney, E. W. Bullard, J. A. Rich, and Benj. H. Brown, were chosen to nominate the committee of fifteen at a subsequent meeting, and the meeting adjourned to the 15th inst., at 2 o'clock, P. M.

At the adjourned meeting the nominating committee reported the following names for the general committee of fifteen: Rev. E. W. Bullard, Joseph Raymond, Benj. H. Brown, Jarvis Davis, John N. Bartlett, Russell Morse, Jr., Cyrus B. Reed, Wellington White, Cyrus Davis, Arba Sherwin, John M. Upham, Edmund Stockwell, Timothy Clark, Joseph L. Perkins, and Maynard Partridge.

Also for the Historical Committee of seven, the following

names; Barnett Bullock, Esq., Daniel Davis, John N. Bartlett, Joseph R. Eaton, Chas. H. Newton, Luther Harrington, and Horace Pierce.

These nominations were adopted.

A previous vote, providing for a free collation, was rescinded.

The town voted to fill the blank in recommendation 6, with the words *fifteen hundred*, and then adopted the remaining recommendations.

Thus far the action of the Town.

Immediately upon the adjournment of the Town Meeting, the General Committee organized by the choice of E. W. Bullard, Chairman, and John N. Bartlett, Secretary.

After instructing the Chairman and Secretary to inform the gentlemen, designated to deliver the Address and Poems, of the action of the Town, and invite them to accept their several appointments, the committee adjourned till Dec. 12th, at 6 o'clock, P. M.

From first to last, the committee held fifteen formal meetings; most of which were fully attended, and all earnestly devoted to the business of deliberating, planning and carrying out the proposed centennial, in the spirit contemplated by the Town. Besides these, there were various meetings of sub-committees, and not a little correspondence, consultation, and labor, involving no small amount of time and expense, in order to mature the general plan, arrange the details, and ensure the success of the enterprise entrusted to their charge. But all was cheerfully and gratuitously met, as well by members from the remote parts of the town, as those at the centre. The post of honor proved a post of sevice and personal sacrifice, but with unanimity at the outset and mutual gratulations at the close, the committee accepted the honor, and now offset the service by the general happiness and grateful memories of the Centennial Day.

The principle sub-committees, as finally arranged, consisted of—

A Committee on Finance.—Joseph Raymond, John N. Bartlett, and Russell Morse, Jr.

A Committee on Printing.—E. W. Bullard, Timothy Clark, and A. H. Brown.

A Committee on the Dinner.—Russell Morse, Jr., John M. Upham, Maynard Partridge, and Edmund Stockwell.

A Committee on Music.—Arba Sherwin, Maynard Partridge, and Wellington White.

A Committee on the Platforms, Seats, &c., of the Speaker's Tent. —Joseph Raymond, Joseph L. Perkins, Cyrus Davis, Cyrus B. Reed, and Jarvis Davis.

The matter of special invitation, and reception, was left to the Committee of the Whole, a general circular being furnished for the Press, and 400 copies thereof, done up in a neat and convenient form, distributed among the members for their own use and the accommodation of their neighbors.

In addition to the Orator and Poets chosen by the Town, the committee chose Rev. E. W. Bullard, of Royalston, President, Rev. A. E. P. Perkins, of Ware, Chaplain, Hon. George Whitney, of Royalston, Chief Marshal, and Benj. E. Perkins, Esq., of So. Danvers, Toast Master of the Day.

Letters of acceptance, or the personal acceptance of these positions, were duly received from all these gentlemen, except Samuel C. Gale, of Minneapolis, Minn., who was obliged reluctantly to decline. The services of the Ashburnham Cornet Band, and of the united Choirs of the Town were secured for the Day.

The dinner committee, with the sanction of the General Committee, finally contracted with M. F. Bigelow, of Roxbury, Caterer, to furnish a dinner, as per Bill of Fare specified, providing an ample tent at his own expense, and laying and serving 800 plates for $1600. Complimentary tickets to this dinner were voted to the Orator, Poet, Chaplain, and Toast Master of the Day, their ladies, and the Band. The remaining tickets were put at $2 00 a piece. Col. Whitney offered a suitable site, near his residence, for the erection of the Dinner Tent, which offer was gratefully accepted.

A spacious tent for the Public Exercises was also contracted for, to be put up and furnished under the direction of the sub-committee having that matter in charge, on the beautiful grounds of R. D. Ripley, Esq., immediately north of his residence, leave having been generously accorded.

The Chief Marshal, was requested to select his own Assistant Marshals.

Vice Presidents, and Secretaries of the Day were chosen, whose names will appear below.

Such were the general arrangements adopted by the Centennial Committee.

The Centennial Day, preceded by a stormy evening and night, opened with one of the most perfect summer morns,—dissipating our fears, and realizing all our hopes. All was fresh and beautiful. Royalston stood forth unveiled and radiant, to welcome back her children, and children's children from abroad, and smile approval on all who had come to do her filial honor.

Many were the returning ones, long separated from the scenes of childhood and youth; many the strangers improving this opportunity to make pious pilgrimage to the early homes or graves of their ancestors and friends; many the less personally related who yet came from city and town, attracted by the occasion, and assured of a welcome to our homes, and the pleasures of the day.

At an early hour the Common began to be alive. All the avenues poured in their contributions to swell the multitude. Old acquaintances and friends were constantly meeting. Groups gathered on the streets, and at almost every door, warmly greeting and greeted, and all enthusiastic. The people were all abroad in the pure air, pleased with one another, proud of old Royalston, and grateful for the auspices of such a glorious morning.

At length the notes of Marshal Music sounded the call to the rendezvous in front of the Church, and at about 10 A. M. the grand procession began to form, under the direction of the Chief Marshal, assisted by a large staff of citizens. After brief marching and counter-marching, to the inspiring music of the Band, the gallant Colonel had his thousands "just where he wanted them"—comfortably seated in the Speaker's Tent.— Proceeding to the residence of Mr. Ripley, with a special escort, he received the Speakers and Officers of the Day, with their ladies, and conducted them also to the Tent.

Every movement had been on time, and the mammoth pavilion was in perfect order when the hour for public services arrived.

The Chief Marshal, ascending the platform, introduced the President of the Day.

The President announced the following Vice Presidents and Secretaries, and invited them to their appropriate seats:

Vice Presidents.—Capt Samuel Lee of Templeton, Rev. Ammi Nichols of Braintree, N. H., Hon. Geo. C. Richardson of Cambridge, Benoni Peck, Esq., of Fitzwilliam, N. H., Harrison Bliss of Worcester, Chauncey Peck of Boston, Rev. Henry Cummings of Newport, N. H., Rev. Sidney Holman of Goshen, Rev. Daniel Shepardson of Cincinnati, O., Rev. Ebenezer Cutler of Worcester, Thomas Norton of Portland, Me., James Raymond of Brooklyn, N. Y., and Hon. Davis Goddard of Orange.

Secretaries.—John P. Gregory of Cambridge, and Joseph E. Raymond of Boston.

These announcements made, the Band was called upon for Music.

The Chaplain, Rev. A. E. P. Perkins, being introduced, read appropriate selections of Scripture, and offered prayer.

The President then arose and said:

"Ladies and Gentlemen: I am charged with a welcome for the assembled children and friends of Royalston. It shall be briefly spoken.

Welcome to this Centennial Day! Welcome to these commemorative services! Welcome to the fast rising memories of the past, and the fresh joys of the present hour! Welcome to the reunion of kindred, neighbors and friends, recalled by this occasion to tread once more together the old familiar paths, and recount the varied experiences of life! Welcome to this jubilee, gratefully harmonious with the public joy in the triumph of government and law over treason and rebellion, of unity over disruption, liberty over oppression! Indeed, a redeemed and vindicated country, methinks, welcomes this natal day of a loyal town, gives you joy in the keeping of it, and, with a significance larger than ever before, pledges you security in the possession and enjoyment of the birthright of freemen. And the old flag, too, baptized anew in blood, and consecrated afresh to American liberty and life, welcomes you to this festival beneath her ample and glorified folds. She, too, remembers the sires, whose counsel and courage gave her birth; and proudly does she salute the sons, who have now given their voice to say it, and their blood to seal—"Let her be perpetual! Let her remain *entire!*"

We meet to commemorate the history of a hundred years—to recall and honor the names and the deeds, both of the living and the dead, that have made this history worthy of commemoration.

A hundred years ago, and these hills and valleys were covered with the primeval forest; these streams, streamlets, and waterfalls wasted their song, as did the wild flowers their sweetness upon the desert air. All was a waste of Nature, awaiting some plastic hand to evoke her latent powers, and bid the wilderness rejoice.

A hundred years have past since the advent of that hand; and to-day the air is full of the memories, and our eyes behold the substantial records of what that hand has wrought.

To give these memories tongue, these records form, and beauty, and enduring life, is the grateful office of the hour.

I felicitate you in gifted sons, able and willing to discharge the sacred trust,—a Bullock, upon whose lips the college, senate and people alike, delighted hang, and to honor whom with her highest gift the commonwealth impatient waits; and a Bryant, early smitten with the love of song, and still allegiant to that early love.

You wait to hear them; and I, not less eager, this welcome spoken, give place to their labors of filial love and fraternal entertainment."

The united choirs of the town now sang, to the tune of "Auld Lang Syne," led by Geo. F. Miller, the following original Hymn, written for the occasion.

BY MRS. GEORGE WOODBURY, OF ROYALSTON:

The memr'y of a hundred years,
   Unfolds its scattered page,
And welcomes back, with grateful tears,
   A past, and present age.
We welcome, now, the good old day,
   Whence gleamed a rising sun,
To guide our footsteps in the way
   That echoes back "well done."

The Red-man's feet had wandered here,
   Where first our grandsires trod;
Their hearts were filled with hope and fear—
   Their firmest trust was God.
That hand still leads and guides us on
   When brighter days illume:
And "home, sweet home," is now our song,
   While pæans swell the tune.

Amid the nodding forest pines,
   Their homes a shelter found,
Where now we train the clustering vines,
   And broad, green fields abound.
Then welcome, welcome, ever more
   The names, our hearts enshrine,
And while we count their hardships o'er,
   Join all in "Auld Lang Syne."

We greet, with joy, this hallow'd day,
   Sweet impress of the past;
'Twill ever shed a ling'ring ray,
   Time will not soon outlast.
We greet you friends, we greet you now,

Who claim a birth-right here,
Though age has marked the earnest brow,
And silvered locks appear.

We welcome back the young and old,
The statesman, priest and sage,
And seal a friendship, tried and told,
That changes not with age.
We sing a requiem for the dead,
Our mem'ries still retain,
And on their graves our tears will shed
While our short lives remain.

We welcome back a hundred years,
And breathe a gentle sigh,
That mingles with our hopes, and fears,
'Mid changes ever nigh.
Soon will another century end,
Earth's dearest ties be riven,
Then may these hearts, which sweetly blend,
Sing with one voice in Heaven.

Following this Hymn, came the Commemorative Address, by the Hon. Alexander H. Bullock.

Mr. Bullock's address, as delivered, occupied about one hour and a half; and held the undivided attention of his large audience to the last. Very much was expected of him; but no one could take in that sea of expressive faces, during any part of the discourse, and doubt that expectation was more than realized. A style and manner so happily adapted to the theme and the occasion, such hearty good will, and filial tenderness breathing through the whole performance, — so much, both of beauty and of worth, drawn from the simple story of a rural town, far back in the interior, and all made so real and important, and so naturally suggesting the eloquent and instructive sentiments with which the orator varied and enriched his discourse, could not fail to satisfy the largest anticipation.

Considerable portions of the written address were not spoken. The whole, however, will be found in the body of this volume. Nor will it suffer, as the speeches of some men must always suffer, by being transferred from the rostrum to the printed page.

After the Address, the Band again discoursed sweet music.

The Poet of the Day, Mr. Albert Bryant, now came forward, and delivered a Commemorative Poem, entitled "Memorials and Garlands," which will be found immediately after the printed Address; and will add to the interest and value of these pages, as its delivery added pleasure and finish to the public exercises.

These exercises closed by the choir and audience uniting in singing, to the immortal "Old Hundred," the 117th Psalm, L. M.

> From all who dwell below the skies,
> Let the Creator's praise arise;
> Let the Redeemer's name be sung,
> Through every land, by every tongue.
>
> Eternal are thy mercies, Lord;
> Eternal truth attend thy word;
> Thy praise shall sound from shore to shore,
> Till suns shall rise, and set, no more.

The Chief Marshal now re-formed the procession, and marched to the Dinner Tent, where about 800 guests sat down to tables tastefully spread and adorned, and beautifully crowned with the substantials, and luxuries of the season.

A blessing was craved by the chaplain. After the feast had been discussed to the apparent satisfaction of all, the President called the company to order, and introduced the Toast Master, Benj. C. Perkins, Esq., whose sentiments, and the hearty responses elicited by them, rounded out the festival, and left nothing more for the consummation of our anniversary, than the reluctant partings, and the garnering of its grateful memories.

We extract the closing paragraphs of a notice of our centennial, which appeared in the Barre Gazette:

"The President of the United States"—was responded to by the band—with—"When Johnnie comes marching home." Edwin Pierce of New York responded for the "Sons of Royalston;" Geo. Richardson of Cambridge,"for the metropolis;" Hon. Artemas Lee of Templeton, "for Worcester county;" Rev. Mr. Marvin of Winchendon, for "our sister towns;" the choir—in a piece of ancient music—for "ye olden time;" Mr. Gregory of Chicago, for "the west;" Rev. Mr. Perkins of Ware, for "the clergy;" the band for "the battle-fields of our country;" with the "Star Spangled Banner;" Rev. Sidney Holman for "the school-masters;" Rev. Mr. Woodworth for "the fellows who stole the hearts of our daughters;" the choir for "the flag of Sumpter;" and closed with Auld Lang Syne.

The music by the Ashburnham Band was truly soul-stirring, and the singing, under the direction of Mr. George F. Miller, was excellent, and both contributed materially to the enjoyment of the occasion. Great credit is also due to the efficiency and promptness of the chief marshal, Hon. Geo. Whitney, for the general good order which prevailed. It was evident that the committee of arrangements and citizens generally had spared no efforts to make the occasion agreeable to all, and the result showed how entirely successful those efforts had been. Altogether it was an occasion to be long and pleasantly remembered by the multitude who were present.

A public meeting of the citizens of Royalston, was notified and held in the Town Hall, on the 2d of September, following the Centennial, with reference to publishing the doings of the day.

Barnett Bullock, Esq. was chosen Moderator, and John N. Bartlett, Secretary of the meeting.

The following "Preamble and Resolutions" were reported, discussed and adopted.

"Whereas it is the duty of the present to commemorate the past, and transmit the deposits of history to the future; and whereas the preparation for, and the results of, our recent centennial have brought together varied and important materials, and the close of the first and the opening of the second century of the incorporate life of Royalston, affords the fitting occasion, therefore,

Resolved, 1. That we, citizens of this town, convened in public meeting to consider this matter, will take immediate measures to secure the compilation and publication of the history of Royalston.

Resolved, 2. That a committee of three be chosen to carry the above resolution into effect as speedily as possible.

Resolved, 3. That the history proposed should be comprised in an octavo volume of from 150 to 200 pages, bound in a neat and substantial, but not expensive binding, and that the copies printed should not exceed 500.

Resolved, 4. That we highly appreciate the Commemorative Address and Poem, pronounced on the occasion of the recent centennial of the town; and that we instruct the Moderator of this meeting to tender our thanks to their authors, and request a copy of each for publication.

Resolved, 5. That we gratefully acknowledge the services of the Historical Committee of the town, in investigating our records, and gathering our reminiscences; and respectfully request the gentlemen composing that committee to co-operate with us in giving completeness and permanence to their labors."

The committee, under the 2d resolution, was filled by the choice of Rev. E. W. Bullard, Daniel Davis, and Joseph R. Eaton.

ADDRESS

OF

Hon. Alex. H. Bullock.

ADDRESS

OF

ALEXANDER H. BULLOCK.

NATIVES AND RELATIVES OF ROYALSTON, FRIENDS AND FELLOW CITIZENS:

Under this spacious awning, on this church lawn and training field of the fathers, we have assembled to commemorate the birthday of our native town.* After the lapse of a century from its first chartered existence, when the men who made the beginning have so long rested from their labors that the same mould of time has gathered over their names and over their dust, and their heroic courage and christian endurance have been partially forgotten for the want of annals, and this rolling territory has passed out of its forest infancy into the maturity of cultured fields, ample dwellings, and an elevated social life, we meet, not so much for the recital of a scanty history, as to indulge the e-motions of the anniversary, and to bid the next generations hail ! And yet, whatever the contrast may be of the past with the present, this hour witnesses the homage of a people plain like their ancestors, among whom the conventionalities of civilization

—*See Appendix. Note A.

have introduced but little of artificial rule, or thought, or custom of life,—around whom the hills and valleys still echo the ancient simplicity. Our home and birth-place offers no boast of the early or later days. Our town has only moved, without eclat, in the paths of an hundred years of allegiance to Christ and the state,—has without pretence to fame responded to every requisition of peace and war,— has constantly kept its step, sometimes feebly, but at all times according to its ability, to the marches of public growth and enterprise, until in the grand results of this day it appears in the sisterhood of the municipalities asking no higher renown than to be credited with having been in every emergency honest, truthful, and faithful. The just man can rest upon such a foundation; the just town can erect its centennial banner upon a ground so simple and broad as that. With such claim to historical justice and historical participation this ancient municipality now calls us all back under the shade of her roof-tree; and we are proudly satisfied to celebrate the day.

I have alluded to the paucity of our annals. The records of the town are considerably meagre, inexplicit, and unsatisfactory. Many reasons might possibly be assigned for this, but that which seems to be most conclusive, is also most creditable to this community. The town, the church, has from the beginning been exempt from those civil and ecclesiastical controversies which have left upon the records of most other communities of New England, full and voluminous materials for history. I find nothing of that sort in your public chest. The life and action of these generations here has been so peaceful and so regular that the clerk has had little to enter upon his book. I apprehend that scarcely an ancient town of the state can present a parallel with this. Such has been the uniformity, the harmony, the serenity of this smooth current of population, from the commencement until now, that the present occasion is furnished with little that is eventful and with nothing that is dramatic. A town far away from the sea, and therefore without the inspiring excitement of ocean commerce,—a precinct that bears no vestiges of the aborigines, and is in this respect so unlike the more southerly towns, which had half a century of life crowded with Indian traditions, that I cannot find that those original lords ever lighted a pipe or a fire here,—a church without a schism in a century,—a ministry that never knew how to quarrel,—a people that have walked the paths of unambitious duty; these make our record uninteresting for the public address. But these also make our claim to the highest distinction of municipal fame. This equable progress of four generations, without anything that is startling in savage or civilized adventure, has made our history comparatively tame; but it is the tameness of beneficence, of a people who have been content without observation to pour the ceaseless tributaries of a small and distant town into the swelling volume of the growth, the power, and the renown of the state.

And yet, simple and unpretending as is the connection of this town with the origin and development of the whole of America, the founders of these local habitations were allies and partakers in the great scheme of the settlement of a new world. The fathers under this charter were of the fathers of the last chapter of civilization. In accordance with the law of colonization their names share the radiance of the sun from the east. They moved under the star of empire to glorious co-operation in the possession of the noblest inheritance of the race. The municipalities of Massachusetts have an honor altogether their own as a part of the instrumentalities which have borne the standard of christian republicanism to the western limits of the continent. Our own ancestors had a share in that blessed lineage, and in that dark and bloody experience of a century and a half, of which this age enjoys the marvellous fruition. The divine beauty of the present has come to us out of the inappreciable sufferings of the past. The angel choirs which have accompanied the divinity of modern liberty, which sang amid the sighing pines around Geneva, and chanted as escort to a representative state and a representative church in the first settlement of this ancient colony, and sweetened those first years of want and famine, and pestilential terrors, have passed over these fields in their coming. All the days of the puritans, all the scenes of their pilgrimage,—Plymouth out of Leyden, Massachusetts Bay out of Plymouth, all the towns of Worcester North out of Massachusetts Bay,—from the landing on the rock to the war of King Philip, thence to the French wars, and onward to the revolution, and the constitution and all the glories under it — over the long track, everywhere, it is a unity, a connection, one providence, one succession, one agency, in which they who lighted their camp fires in the face of Indians in Lancaster and Brookfield, and they who cleared fields in the presence of wild beasts in Templeton and Royalston were pursuing a common destiny for the success of a republican church and an American liberty. And so we have a part to-day with the founders of the New England polity, whose mark is over the whole continent.

There was a natural order in the settlement of these towns. English colonization in America wisely adopted the sea-board as its base, and extended its operations to the interior. In this order of the possession and clearing of the country our own town came late, being more remote than any other in the county from the seminal sources of the state. Some of the towns in the southerly part of the county were occupied by the Anglo-American an hundred years earlier than this. Indeed, of the entire territory of Worcester county, as the same was disposed of by grants and charters, our own town is the junior of all by many years; for although our neighbors, Templeton and Athol, were both incorporated on the same day, only about three years before us, and Winchendon preceded us by only a single year of its charter, yet, as to all those towns, grants of lands and settlements had been made much earlier, varying from twenty to thirty years. The wave of occupation seemed to pause immediately below our border for some years. This being frontier territory, an outside row was left for a long time unplanted. Nor was this fact without its advantages; for though our late coming into the family of charters has cut us off from some of the excitements of early traditions, which I greatly appreciate as stimulations to public character, it gave to the early settlers here the benefits of the maturity of the posessions surrounding them. So that while the first occupants of Athol were obliged to maintain a garrison against the Indians who had kept a seat there to a late day, the triumph and success which followed was appropriated to the security of the first comers in Royal-shire. But the special advantage of coming after our sisters of the county is better illustrated by the fact that the novitiate of colonization, the *interim* between settlement and municipality, was thus made so brief that between the first planting and the first fruit there was scarcely an appreciable space of time; for, while it occurred in other parts of this county that thirty and forty years elapsed after settlement before municipal incorporation, that intervening period was represented here by only the interval of three years. These lands were scarcely known as a value to the first shrewd proprietors at Boston before the town itself took a place in the provincial records as a living community, a political power, a participator in the fortunes of the commonwealth. Thus there was no infancy here; it was robust manhood from the start.

The territory of this town has undergone many changes, and indeed was a subject of some uncertainty at the outset.* June 4, 1752, a vote was approved in Council ordering a sale of the lands north of Pequoig, now Athol, and onward to the province line. The purpose was to clear the map; and so effectually was this accomplished, that the surveyor's chain swept in a strip of several miles in length lying along the whole northern boundary of Winchendon, separating it from the province line, which had been inadverdently omitted in the survey of that town; and this was afterwards called the *Royalston leg*. For obvious reasons the limb proved an incumbrance, and was severed in 1780, when these many acres which had come to us like an estray, were transferred to Winchendon. Under the sovereignty of our king, the township was sold at public vendue. This form of procedure, under which the country itself had been ceded by charters and was afterwards parcelled out, was a part of that policy which, following up the law of discovery and conquest by internal settlement and improvement, has made England the great power of the earth, under which she even now plants her
—*Note B.

authority and extends her civilization alike in India and in North America. The purchasers and first proprietors of our town were men of exalted names and characters. And although they were proprietors only, not settlers, yet I cannot doubt that association with so much of fame and virtue left impressions of manliness and honor upon those who came and remained here. Samuel Watts, Thomas Hubbard, ISAAC ROYAL, James Otis, Isaac Freeman, and others, for the consideration of £1348, took the title to 28,357 acres, exclusive of former private grants. These grants, amounting to 1700 acres, are known in the archives at the State House as Pierpont's, Priest's and Hapgood's. In accordance with the wise policy of the government of that day,— a policy which has been continued by the general government since our independence in every time of war, and at no time so liberally as in our recent conflict with the Rebellion,—the sovereign power had bestowed these grants as bounties for military services rendered. I call them military services, for such they were, whether rendered in the field or at home in support of the field. The name attached to one of these grants has become a part of the local geography and daily life of the town. Priest, who received 300 acres as a recognition of his loyalty in extending the hospitality of his half-way house near the easterly line of the town to all those who passed that way to and from the French wars, will ever live in the beautiful river which bears his name. And so long as the calm flow of its waters shall continue, so long shall live the memories of that service which associates your town with the pioneers and the rangers, with the Lily of France, with Louisburg, with that fidelity to the crown of our king in those days which I cannot but like, with those wars for our royal Georges which prepared and educated our fathers afterward to overwhelm all kings in the Revolution.

I have lived in this town long enough to have learned that in the trade of land we can calculate as closely as other men; and let me remind you that we inherit the talent from an honorable ancestry. I find in the Massachusetts Archives, volume 46, that these same Watts, Royal, and Otis at length discovered that as far back as 1737 the Court had made a private grant of 600 acres to Benoni Moore and others, afterwards assigned to one Hunt and thenceforward known under his name, and that the location had been taken by him in the very heart of the best land, 200 acres of which, however, had somehow been relinquished; whereupon they claimed other acres as good somewhere else in the Province, or an equivalent relief. Certainly this seemed a very plausible land claim, and the allowance was voted. Subsequently, it appears by the report of a Committee, that after the allowance of the claim, a correct survey disclosed that these proprietors had originally taken 500 acres more than their deed expressed, and more than they paid for, leaving them quite largely in debt to the Province; which I cannot see that they ever made good, though probably the advantage does not inure to any present landholder of Royalston.

And so your town began under a territorial proprietorship of 30,577 acres, the private grants included. In 1780 the unmanageable leg, estimated at about 2000 acres, was set off to Winchendon. In 1783 several thousand acres were appropriated to Orange, when that town was incorporated. In 1799, 300 or 400 acres were added from Athol and Gerry (now Phillipston.) In 1803 several hundred acres were added from Athol. In

1837 not far from 200 acres were taken out of Phillipston, and annexed to your jurisdiction.

The title and charter muniments, therefore, now assign to this municipality not far from 26000 acres.* It has the disadvantage of remoteness from the sea and of a northern frontier contiguity, which is considerable; but it enjoys the compensations of a soil submissive to cultivation, rigorous to the sight, but yielding generously to the stroke of the earnest arm,—of benignant drifts and ranges,—of the affluent waterfalls of Miller's and Priest's rivers, and of the simpler Lawrence and Tully, which give richness because they give plenty,—of rural beauty, worthy of historic record, at the Royal falls of Forbes and of Doane,—of the sparkling mineral gems which the official geologist of Massachusetts once told me he had gladly set in his family seal, —of an atmosphere that inspires youth and enlivens age,†—of territorial possessions, simple indeed, but glistening with the authority of the names of the fathers of American Independence, —of a planting in the mountain air, of a history studded with patriotic associations, of a religious connection that shall bear your children to the heights of a happy remembrance of the names of their fathers,—of a place on the sweet, broad plain of this civilization of Worcester North, stars encircling overhead, and a simple robustness of character sustaining the people.

And so you will adhere to the territorial vestments dropped upon you and around you by your ancestors, clinging to your acres and yielding them not to other calls. Your town is symmetrical and compact, large enough and small enough, and bears a just proportion to the prescriptive idea of a Massachusetts

—* **Note B.**
—† **Note C.**

township of six miles square. I would not diminish it nor enlarge it. Let other municipalities nibble around your borders, but let them nibble in vain, and you will hold fast to that which is good, and which is none too much.

And now if we revert to the proceedings of these purchasers of our soil, we discover from their journals that they held proprietors' meetings from 1753 over a period of thirty-four years, until 1787, when their records were closed and sealed*. To James Otis, Isaac Royal, and their original associates, John Hancock was added as an owner in 1765. No town can assert a better beginning or a more reputable heritage of name and blood. The proprietors held their meetings in Boston, "at the Bunch of Grapes Tavern." At the first meeting it was "motioned that the land aforesaid be called Royal-shire, and they unanimously agreed thereto, whereupon the Hon. Isaac Royal generously gave his word to give the Partners £25 sterling, towards building a meeting-house for said town." Here we first find our name.

The Hon. Isaac Royal was a citizen of Medford, a gentleman of great spirit for public enterprise, devoted in admiration for his king, and generous and munificent for his time. He was a member of the General Court and of the Council for twenty-two years. The pulpit Bible which was used in this First Congregational society for seventy-five years, was a gift from him.— He also gave two thousand acres, a large part of which was in this town, to found the professorship of law in Harvard University which still bears his name. He promised to give a full lot of land in this township to the first male child that should be born here, but several girls taking the precedence of birth,

—*Note D.

Royal Chase, named after him, came too late on the stage, and died too early, to make the proffer availing. For, in the meantime, the elements of the Revolution gathered and broke, and our benefactor and friend, Isaac Royal, who could not give up his king, passed over to the tories, sailed for England in 1776, and never returned. It is related in the history of the refugees that after his departure even his beautiful estate at Medford refused cultivation, that the scythe relucted to cut tory grass, and the oxen to plough tory soil. The tone of his letters from England in 1779, written before Independence was by any means assured, indicated his yearning desire to return to Massachusetts, and to make his last bed by the side of his relatives and friends. But the desire came too late, for by the sweeping act of October 16, 1778, passed by the House of Representatives, and approved in Council, he whose name we hear, received the indelible character of an exile and an outlaw.* But let not that which was a political necessity of the time perpetuate his reproach; and this, I perceive, was the judgment of our fathers. No town was more patriotic than this in the Revolution; but I rejoice that its citizens appear never for one moment to have thought of giving up their corporate name because their benefactor had estranged himself from their political opinions. The name of this town and the title of the Cambridge law professorship may honorably be retained in his remembrance.

The first possession of this soil by our ancestors dates from 1752, but the French war of 1756 — the most dramatic and engrossing contest on this continent prior to that of the Revolution — threw all the arts and labors of peaceful enterprise

—*Note D.

into suspense and abeyance for several years. You will appreciate how and why the clearing and culture of the globe was suspended here to make way for the practice of the bayonet, if you recall that the whole population of the province was drawn into the vortex of that war. Not in the Revolution, not in the late Rebellion of which the pressure is still heavy on your hearts, were the young men, who settle the land, so disproportionately called into the field of arms. In that conflict of seven years we are informed that Massachusetts alone sent to the field thirty-five thousand of her sons, and seven thousand for each of three successive years. Every nook and corner of this province was exhausted by the universal call.

As the war approached its end the permanent settlement of these lands began. In sympathy with the policy of the fathers of New England, the proprietors of Royal-shire laid our foundations in moral and mental education. At their first meeting in 1753 they had directed the land to be laid off into 60 lots for settlers, and three others for a minister, for the support of worship, and for a school. Their committee came here and personally superintended this work, and selected the wild spot so familiar to us on the Lawrence stream for the mills. The church and the school, the saw mill and the grist mill, were the early handmaids of our civilization. They are so to this day in the West, beyond the Mississippi, where our example is repeated. In 1761, the war having spent its fury, deeds had been granted to twenty-one settlers. In the next year these ten acres near which you have pitched your pavilion were solemnly consecrated for the meeting house, the training field, and the burial ground, —the last of which was subsequently by exchange removed a little farther to the South, out of what is now this comely village; and a contract was made for the mills.

In the following year, 1763, a meeting house was contracted for at two hundred pounds, which was completed in 1764.— Still another year witnessed the prompt execution of the wise policy of the founders, in setting apart 231 acres for the first minister, 424 acres for the ministry, and 420 acres for the school. To procure sixty settlers the proprietors offered to each man one hundred acres, with the condition of settling a clergyman, clearing six acres, and building every one a house. No higher wisdom than this ever initiated a town or a state.— And then the remaining lots were divided among the proprietors by drawing; and that was the profit which they deserved.*

In this year, 1765, February 16th, the act of incorporation of the town, under the name of Royalston, was approved in Council. No copy of the act appears among your files. Accordingly I have availed myself of the kindness of the present obliging Secretary of State, Hon. Oliver Warner, and have procured a literal transcript of the charter, handsomely engrossed upon parchment and bearing his attestation, which the town clerk will please faithfully preserve. It is the titular charter of the last and youngest of all the towns of this ancient and noble County in the days of the province and of the royal arms. It is worthy of preservation, for under it your fathers have kept the public name untarnished, and you will see to it that no blemish shall alight upon the life of the present generation.†

The active settlement of this town began in 1762, when six families moved in, some of whose blood still circulates among

—*Note F.
—†Note G.

your residents. I think we may estimate highly the soundness of the stock of these sturdy pioneers, since it appears the average age of these six heads at their death was not less than 76 years. So rapid was the influx of new comers, that almost soon after the French war had closed as many as seventy five heads of families had become established here, many of whose names help to fill your voting list in the present day. Time will not allow me to make use of the long list which is in my hands as I should like. Theirs was a wilderness life under a degree of hardship, of toil and deprivation, which only strong arms and hearts valiant in Christian faith could have sustained.

No imagination of this day, no preserved traditions of the past, can do justice to those early labors. Many of these men who came hither from Sutton, as was illustrated in the instance of Capt. Sibley, would clear a piece of wood-land here, go back to look after haymaking in Sutton, and return in time to sow a rye-field in Royalston. Prior to the erection of the first mill by Isaac Gale, bags of grain were carried on the shoulders of men to a neighboring town to be ground and brought back in the same manner. No wonder that they who thus opened the pathway in this town with humble means, and patient labor, were the same that confronted boldly James Otis and John Hancock, a committee of the proprietors, and insisted before the legislature upon the justice and equity of taxing the lands of non-residents for the support of the Gospel; and no wonder that they succeeded against even those overshadowing names. I desire not to appear invidious in selecting out of so many who were prominent in their day.* The three Selectmen chosen at the first town meeting May 7th,

—* Note II.

1765, John Fry, Timothy Richardson, and Benj. Woodbury, bore names which have descended in other representatives of their blood through the records of a century, and which still live in honor and respect among you. The limitations of my address will only permit an allusion to the first of these.

John Fry, a lineal descendant in the 5th generation of one who came from England and settled in this country, moved from Sutton to Royalston and resided on yonder eminence. He was called here the Esquire, but he brought with him a distinction of arms. I have had placed at my use by one of his kinsmen the original commission under the king which he received as first Lieutenant from Gov. Shirley in 1745, and under which he fought before Louisburg and entered the fort to the music of the same drums which thirty years later beat still better sounds at Bunker Hill. Ten years afterwards he bore royal commission as Captain for service at Crown Point. He was past the time for military activity when the Revolution opened, and was obliged to suppress his soldierly instincts in the home life of a good deacon and model citizen. He lived here nearly fifty years, and died at ninety-six.

As I look over the memoranda concerning those men of the last century which have been gathered from traditions and placed in my hands, my admiration is excited for their endurance and their whole character. It was the best of stock with which to build up a town. I have also been impressed by the uniform fact of their remarkable longevity which attests the purity and contentment of their lives. For small gains, but many large and virtuous rewards, they struggled manfully in the infancy of American civilization; they drove out wild beasts and subdued the wilderness;* they opened the paths to a better condition for those who came after them, to more comfortable homes and a larger affluence; worn out at last they lay down to their rest in the track their own hands had made, and they left to the present generation a heritage of works in which all ages may discern the beauty and the strength of Religion, Subordination, and Patriotism.

Aided by the munificence of Col. Royall the proprietors erected the first meeting house in 1764 near the centre of this public ground.†

It was left in a rude state of unfinished interior and without pews. Upon one side of the broad aisle were seated the males and upon the other the females, as was then usual in country houses of worship, which custom appears to have continued during a period of nearly forty years. There being no distinctive seats assigned to the singers, the tuning-fork and deaconing off by lines came to the rescue of church harmony. Thirty-three years after, in 1797, the old house was removed, and another more commodious took its place. This remained with some alterations till it was destroyed by fire in 1851 when the present appropriate edifice was reared. These changes have been very marked and the contrast is striking. I can conceive that if John Fry, Timothy Richardson, and Benjamin Woodbury were to come back in the flesh and be ushered along the present aisles and by darkened windows, to carpeted slips and cushioned seats, and this new organ‡ of yours were to practice upon their ears the imitation of a few of its flutes and its fiddles, and

—* Note I.
—† Note J.
—‡ NOTE.—The gift of Mrs. Emily Bullock Ripley to the First Congregational Society.

should wind up with a swell or two of the grand diapason, they would call upon their leader of 1765 to draw the sword which he flashed at Crown Point, and to drive out of the house a congregation of worshippers who could tolerate such innovations. But we must remember that each age has its standard, and that in nothing else do men become so sacredly attached to their custom as in matters relating to Christian worship.

I have spoken of the first condition imposed by the proprietors upon the landholders. that they should support a minister. During the first three years of incorporation, the temporary services of several clergymen were secured, but it is not important to recite their names. At length, in April, 1768, the town extended a call to the Rev. Joseph Lee to settle. You will bear in mind that this was then what has been since termed by the Courts a poll-parish, the town and the religious society blending under the law. He was offered for settlement £400 "old tenor." in addition to the 231 acres granted by the proprietors for the first settled minister, and in lawful money a salary of £46, 13s., 4d., per annum for the first three years, £53, 6s., 8d., per annum for the next three years, and £60 each year thereafter, and thirty cords of wood to be drawn annually from his own land to his door.

The church of sixteen persons had been formally organised two years before. The call was accepted and the pastoral office was filled by ordination Oct. 19th, 1768. His life, his services, his eulogy are in the dim letters upon that familiar tablet-stone in the neglected grave yard, which time will soon render illegible, unless you shall chisel them or color them anew.

Mr Lee was born in Concord, May 12th, 1752. graduated at Harvard college in 1765, and died here February 16th, 1819. He preached to this people fifty years and his half century sermon was his last. I count it the most fortunate of all the events of your history that a man of good qualities by nature, and of university education took his lot with the early settlers and directed the conscience and judgment of the first two generations of the town. To the steadiness and unity of the influences of that long and patient pastorate I ascribe largely the exemption from violent tendencies which has marked this community,—the uninterrupted, straight forward, placid career of Royalston. The exhortations to the society for peace and harmony, contained in the concluding passages of the half century discourse, were simply the expression in language of his own half century of pastoral and benignant life.

His spare form, in the style of the old school, emerging through that garden gate year in and year out with scrupulous punctuality to the church service, wearing authority meekly, yet as consciously as one of the oriental fathers,—his eccentricities, incapable of disguise, but so repressed as not to detract from his influence—his genial participation in the rural sociability of that period of simplicity,—his scholarly culture, not the most extensive, but held at good command and use,—his humor, offset by his gravity;—his tact flexibility at not passing the bounds of his sincerity;—these are only the outlines of the picture which brings before us the parson of one half of your entire historic existence. I regret that my personal memory does not extend back to the time of his death; but it is my pleasure to speak words of tribute to his memory. If each generation of men in

New England could have *forty* such men as Lee in Royalston, Estabrook in Athol, and Sabin in Fitzwilliam, the towns and the churches would live in perpetual peace.

The order of topics, rather than of chronology, demands the completion of my notice of this society. Three months before his death, being then seventy-six years old, feeble and infirm, Mr. Lee turned his attention to the thought of a colleague and successor. On the last day of November, 1818, he called his church around him, in his long accustomed chair, under his own roof. A day of public fasting and prayer was appointed in which the congregation united in December, when those two brothers of peace, Sabin and Estabrook, conducted the services; immediately after which the church made unanimous choice of Ebenezer Perkins as associate pastor. The invitation was accepted by the young divine, and the Council for ordination assembled on the 17th day of February, 1819, at the house of Joseph Estabrook, which, according to the stability of things here, I am happy to say, is still the residence of son. The venerable senior pastor had expired only a few hours before, and his closed lips spoke in the eloquence of silence the most impressive lesson of that day.

Mr. Perkins continued as pastor twenty-eight years, when, chiefly for reasons arising from the state of his health, he requested dismissal. He retained the respect and confidence of the whole town throughout his life, and died in this town of his adoption and love. My earliest recollection of church-going are associated with his fine personal form, his full voice, his free and dignified delivery, his style of public prayer, which for mingled solemnity and facility it has rarely been my lot to hear surpassed. He was a native of Essex county, and a graduate of Dartmouth College. Gravity of demeanor was his rule of public appearance, but as I knew him in private he was one of the most social and agreeable of gentlemen. He came here a mere youth, to succeed one who left behind the veneration belonging to an official life of half a century, and it is but justice to his memory to say that not one out of a thousand men would have succeeded so well and left a better record in the town.

The third minister, Norman Hazen, was settled in June, 1847. —a young man of superior education, but of a slender body laboring under disease. At the end of five years his ministry terminated with his life. I knew him somewhat, and can freely say that his term here seemed a constant triumph of the spiritual over the mortal. The appeal of his life was a continued pathos, and the pathos of his death was greater.

His successor, Ebenezer W. Bullard, was installed September 2d, 1852, and still remains. May he, like his predecessors, abide among you until his death. But I am not to speak of the living to day.

And yet a word more to the first Congregational Society. One of its late members, no longer among the living,[*] who, after the struggle and poverty of his youth, worshipped with you in peace for nearly fifty years to the day of his death, four weeks before he died, subscribed to a legacy to this parish, which I must be pardoned for calling liberal. In sympathy with the spirit of James Otis and Isaac Royall he conditioned his bequest upon the continued support of the gospel ministry. I may be permitted to believe that the spirit of the testator will

—[*] The late Hon. Rufus Bullock. See also Note K.

abide with the society,—that in nothing niggardly, or reluctant, or regretful, the large and competent Parish will carry out wisely and liberally the policy of the early proprietors and the recent benefactor. Seed-time and harvest without failure come and go with the years; and they will be most prosperous, most happy, who pull wide the purse-strings in the presence of the ordinances of the Lord.

When Mr. Lee came into the town the Baptists must have numbered nearly one fourth part of the inhabitants;—ten of forty-two families, as he informs us. They organized a church in 1768, two years later than the other, and built between 1774 and 1784 a house of worship on the west bank of the Tully. You will consider that these people had no Boston proprietors to aid them but relied upon their own limited resources and large faith. The manner of their proceeding at that time, so simple, so earnest, so singular, quite wins upon one who will examine their records. In all the time from that day they appear to have settled about twelve pastors, of whom the first was Whitman Jacobs, who continued some eighteen years or more so far as I can learn, and who in my apprehension left here many of those marked and decisive influences which control a local history. He died in this town in 1801. Two of these pastors, Moses Kenney and Isaac Kenney, brothers, died only a little more than a year apart, and were followed to a common sleep "amid the pines under the hill." With one of the later ministers of that church, Mr. Silas Kenney, who labored with success through many years, it was my fortune to serve in the Legislature of the State, where I found him to be the worthy and sound representative of this town.

During the intervals between the pastorates they never gave up religious service. There is something of the simplicity of the oriental time in the way they kept their cause alive. They had the custom, which, it has always seemed to me, must be greatly attractive in the early age of a republican church, of allowing men not ordained to conduct their exercises, if they possessed the gift. Such was the first man who ministered to them. Thus " the brethren by appointment met together to converse with Bro. Rich's improvement among us, and being satisfied that he had a gift to preach the gospel, we desired him still to improve his gift with us." Similar passages appear in their records which have the charm of this novelty, and of unaffected devotion to the christian mission.

After 1800 their old tabernacle disappeared and under the auspices of a union of the Baptists of Royalston and Warwick a large new house was erected near the line between the two towns, which was dedicated in 1805. I suspect that they had sons of thunder in those days, for we are told that upon the occasion of the raising of this meeting-house the prayer of Elder Hodge was heard at the distance of half a mile. This building was condemned in 1847, and rebuilt, and rededicated a mile eastward at a place called " the city."

My brief tribute to the heroic virtues of this class of our people would be imperfect if I were to neglect to render justice to their peaceful disposition. They were large in numbers and of meagre worldly fortune, but without anything of that ill-conceived jealousy which such contrasts are apt to engender. Accordingly their relations with the town and with the first parish over the period of a century, have been conciliatory, honorable and generous. Not another town is known to me in which the relations of the citizens and the churches have been for an hundred years without interruption so harmonious and felicitous. May the next ten decades witness the same happiness of conciliation, and welcome the generations to even a larger glory in the heavens.

In 1837 a second Congregational church was organized at South Royalston, in a large degree by amicable dismissals from the first.

The quite rapid modern growth of that village under the stimulation of its water power on Miller's river had rendered essential better local conveniences for religious fellowship and worship. And now again the dying counsels of father Lee, the counsels of peace, ruled the hour; and the first parish with Mr. Perkins, its pastor, co-operated heartily in this enterprise. The next year Samuel H. Peckham was settled as the first pastor; Neeland, Goodyear and others have followed, the church and society have prospered, and under the probable future of the town this will continue only a secondary institution of ecclesiastical and civil power among the influences that shall make up the destiny of the days of your municipality. The Society has a large and elegant house of worship.

In the same village there is a Methodist society and meeting house, the first in the town. Some preparatory preaching for this dates back to 1827, but the church was not organized until 1842, since which time it has been for the most part continued. I hear of nothing but kindly feelings between the two societies in that section. Neither quarrelsome persons nor quarrelsome churches can have a residence in this town. Joseph

Lee settled that matter a great while ago for his own day, and for many generations after him.

There was at one time a Universalist Society, and what was called a Free Donation Society, which were respectable in numbers and worshipped in school-houses. I have not been able to find their records; but I judge that when, some thirty-three years ago, the third article of the Bill of Rights was so changed as to invest every citizen with the right to contribute to any religious society, or to none at all, according to his volition, this class of organizations disappeared from the town and have left no record behind.

A Union Society, so called, was organized here in 1839, out of a branch of the Baptist Church in the west and some Universalists of Athol. They erected a good looking meeting-house at the southeast corner of these public grounds, where the two denominations alternately controlled the service. That was an abnormal condition of things which could not possibly endure. And so the Baptists at length bought out the property and for some years kept up a church quite large in its numbers, having at one time one hundred and twenty members. But this enterprise was against the public want, accordingly stopped running in 1854, and in 1863 they permitted the house to be sold and moved away;—leaving this common training field and churchyard of our forefathers just as it began an hundred years ago, with one meeting house, whose spire shall always rise to catch the first gilding of the rising sun and to scatter over these hills and valleys the radiance of one patriotic hope, one christian faith, one common destiny. And so this day of the living and the next day of the coming shall echo back response and sympathy to those who gave us the birth-right and then passed to the ages of everlasting rest.

Among the early and arduous trials of this settlement was the construction of roads* for travel. The difficulty was enhanced by the wild and broken features of the country and by the location of the sites for habitations. If you reflect that here was a wilderness, in which men selected prominent points for houses, to which the paths must be made to conform without the skill of modern engineering, the blazing of trees supplying their science, and that communication and transport must be had among the settlers and with the region outside, you apprehend the necessity and the obstacles which confronted them. But in the first year of the charter they resolutely assailed the wild scene around them and with poll bridges and corduroy bottoms made their condition respectable. It would be easy to point out the first four avenues which in 1765 and 1766 were made to radiate from the meeting-house over the hills to the four points of the compass. In 1766 the town adopted the state policy, substantially the same which prevails at this day and which has given the highways of Massachusetts a fame in every part of the country. Great improvements in this direction have characterized the history of this town, which, starting with these four avenues in the early days, has now seventy-five or eighty miles of good highways paying daily tribute to an advanced civilization.

In 1768 the first physician, Stephen Batcheller,† established himself here. Down to the time of his death, in 1829, at the age of eighty-three, he remained here, and illustrated the highest style of fidelity to a life of professional honor and duty. Some

—* Note L.
-† Note M.

of you can remember him as he rode over these paths in his saddle, generally without a girth for greater safety in the accidents of uncertain bridges and byways, with those traditional bags, which were so long recognized as the insignia of his profession. He deserves to be cherished in the combined associations of a lengthened and honored citizenship and of those solemn and tender services which in nearly a half century of practice received the gratitude of the living and took no reproach from the memorials of the dead.

His son, Stephen Batcheller, Jr., practised here and in all the northeastern portions of Massachusetts, nearly as long as he, and with a more widely spread reputation. His education was respectable, but his sagacity and instincts were uncommon and remarkable. Most eminent practitioners in the state, who met him in the conventions of the Faculty at Boston and Worcester, have told me that his rank was of the highest. Who of us does not today recall his portly dimensions, his elastic step, his perceptions of our ailments, his wit and mirth of conversation which palliated the bitterness of the potion he administered and forced convalescence into wholesome jollity? No physician in the county of Worcester ever rode so many miles as he. He practised a little after the old style, but he had grand ideas of common sense about sickness and health. One such Doctor to a generation in a town becomes a far reaching power in the issues of life and death.

He was succeeded by Isaac P. Willis, who served here with positive skill and science in his profession, with great favor among the people of this whole section and died only a few years ago to the great grief of all. His successor who has but recently moved here, is now in the line of distinguished predecessors and benefactors, whose example opens before him a good beginning.

Dr. Thomas Richardson practiced here more than twenty years, residing in the Northeasterly part of the town. He studied for his profession with the late Dr. Carter, (senior,) in Lancaster. A native of Leominster, he came into this town about 1790, at the age of twenty-four. He had a first-class reputation as a physician and a citizen; his practice was quite large, and enabled him to accumulate property. In the later years of his residence here he owned and occupied the Willard Newton place, which he still continued to carry on for a considerable period after his removal from town. He has been less generally known than he would otherwise have been to the present generation of Royalston by reason of his having moved to Fitzwilliam in 1812, where he became a prominent citizen, and was, for a long time, its largest tax-payer; and once at least its representative in the legislature. He had a fine taste and a thorough knowledge in the department of raising horses, in which he stood at the head in this section of the country. He died in 1852, aged 87, ripe in years and crowned with the respect and confidence of his fellow citizens. He was the father of the Hon. George C. Richardson who resided with us here for many years and has since gained a wide reputation as a successful and representative Boston merchant.

The medical gentlemen who have served at South Royalston, have received the confidence of the community. My information does not enable me to go farther in relation to them.

No lawyer was ever settled in this place. The late Mr. Justice Strong of Leominster, I believe, once came here on a professional reconnoisance, but the field not looking promising he left at an early day. The people of the town have not been given to much litigation. Its corner stones were laid in the spirit of peace, and the angel of harmony has presided over every stage of the rising and growing structure.

And now I cannot refrain from felicitating the inhabitants of Royalston over a fact which becomes at this point pertinent and impressive. As to all the central portion of the town, and by far the larger part of its whole population, after the expiration of one hundred years, you start on this second century with only the fourth clergyman and the fourth physician since the origin. This is indeed a striking circumstance. And it has had much to do in forming and sustaining the character of the people. Every thing, stable, tried, approved and held fast,—nothing fitful, violent or rushing,—has entered into the public policy or general life, or private action of this municipality among the hills of the frontier. From father to son, without the intermittent fevers which have racked many other communities, familiarity with the same faces, with the same principles, with the same professional and dominating influences, has descended through the years of a century and made the very name of Royalston a synonym for stability, tranquility and contentment. This is an inheritance to you worth your continued care to preserve.

The patriotic history of the town is in proportion with all its other features. Those early settlements were made amid the rumblings of the approaching Revolution, and your first proprietors were among its chief actors. They divided, and Chandler and

Royal went off to the loyalists. They were better known to our forefathers than were Otis and Hancock at that day, for Royal they cherished as their benefactor, and Chandler had been active and fair in laying out their primeval lands. But they subordinated personal gratitude to public patriotism.

I do not know that there was a single tory among them all. Not even their poverty opened a door to the seductive blandishments of crowns and thrones. They had those among them who had borne the commission of their king and who had fought for his diadem on the line of the ocean and the lake; but they cast all these pleasant memories behind them, waited not to know which side should win, and threw themselves, their town, their all into the breach with the struggling colonists for independence.

Through the town records of the Revolutionary period I find loosely scattered and poorly preserved sufficient proof of the exalted patriotism of those good men. It cannot be necessary that their votes and acts should be here set forth in detail. It appears that a committee of correspondence with the province committee was early chosen; Henry Bond, who lived on the Jonas Bartlett place, was sent delegate to the first Provincial Congress in 1774, and Nahum Green to the second in 1775; in 1776 a committee of safety was appointed and for five years thereafter this committee was as regularly chosen as the legal town officers; in the same year the town deeply interested itself in the question of a State Constitution, which, having been framed at length but imperfectly, received the negative vote of this people and an able argument against it from the pen of Mr. Lee*: frequently were the doings of the Continental Congress

—* Note N.

at Philadelphia read and approved in open meeting here; £90 for bounties were raised in 1778 and the selectmen were instructed to collect clothing and ammunition for the soldiers; in 1779 no family of its own soldiers was found to be needy, and so £42 were voted to each of its citizens engaged in the service two years before; Sylvanus Heminway was chosen the same year to the convention to form a second constitution and the work of instructing him was delegated to a committee of which Mr. Lee was the head; and again in the same year, as a part of the war system and war strength, the people co-operated with the Concord convention to fix the prices of commodities and to diminish the mischief of a depreciated currency*; in 1780 large sums were raised to buy beef and clothing for the army.   And now the old finance was failing and the necessity came of hiring the soldier and paying the clothing and the beef in hard money only, and in 1781 you find the fathers, few and poor as they were, raising more than a thousand pounds in Spanish milled dollars for the hire of soldiers, and voting in addition to each man in the field at the end of three years, "ten cows,—heifers three years old with calf, or with calves by their side."   Point me in a young, poor town to a more liberal patriotism than that. During all this time the first settlers were continually going themselves into the service, the last two men marching off in 1782. There was no call from Philadelphia to which they did not respond, nor a drum-beat heard from Bunker Hill, or Saratoga, or Bennington, with which their hearts did not keep music.— When Burgoyne in the North spread abroad such terror the

—* Note O.

men of this town and of all northern Worcester rose to arms and marched forth for the encounter. All this occurred when more than half these acres were covered with the original forests, when the settlements were in their infancy, when the currency was perplexing all the relations of life, and when Royalston had only between six hundred and seven hundred inhabitants. Other and older and richer towns did more, but I humbly submit that none did better than this.

It is a source of increasing regret that the records of the town in its primitive period have only partially preserved the names of their Revolutionary soldiers. From the books, imperfectly kept as they were, I derive the names of Nahum Green, Samuel Barton, Squier Davis, John Whittemore, Nathaniel Jacobs, Timothy Armstrong, Michael French, Roger Chase, Moses Walker, Joel Stockwell, Eliphalet Richardson, B. Woodbury, Eleazer Burbank, Bezaleel Barton, Isaac Nichols, and Silas Cutting. Others there were, many and as good, but their names have not been saved. The last named of these was one of the first six settlers of the town in 1762, and died in the military service of the war. But the remainder of them had come here a little later than 1762, in the shoal or drift of settlers who floated in this direction so rapidly from the Southern towns. One of them, Nahum Green, was the delegate to the second Provincial Congress of Massachusetts in February, 1775. He appears to have gone from that Congress into the first army gathered for Independence at Charlestown, and was probably engaged in the battle of Bunker Hill; he returned here in July and died of the small pox, which he had contracted while in the service.   This first martyr which Royalston contributed to the Revolution, was privately buried near his own home about a mile southerly of this spot, and the soldiers resting place can now barely be identified by the remaining cobbles that make his headstone.   Cannot this town afford by some simple, appropriate and enduring memorial, to rescue from oblivion the gory bed of the aboriginal patriot whose name yet survives without a tablet the scene of the first mortal sacrifice offered in her behalf to the immortality of the American Union?   Pardon me for asking you to think of this and to act either by private subscription or in open town meeting.   Another of them, Nathaniel Jacobs, as it appears, unintentionally, in the quaint language of the papers in your chest, "did a tower of duty in Rhode Island." All of these, and many others whose names are lost to our sight, struggled throughout the conflict, and some died in the battles, that they might write the honor of their young municipality upon the shining bosses of the Republic of the world in the West. And I am proud to be able to stand before you and to say that of all who enlisted into that service from this town not one, not one, was ever recorded as a deserter.   We meet to day upon their ancient training ground to render ascriptive gratitude for the honor of their robust virtues, for the example of their marvellous sacrifices, for the fame of their glorious death.   Let us in our day cherish the memories of our ancestors in that war, and transmit every syllable of their names encircled with reverence to the last posterity.*

At the close of the Revolution our forefathers initiated the wise policy of equity in averaging the great cost of the war upon the

—* Note P.

whole population. You have within the present year adopted the principle which they inaugurated and have averaged the cost of the late Rebellion in the same manner. This was public justice then, and it is public justice now. Many other towns attempted the same thing at that time, and abandoned it; but here it was carried out successfully. I find that Captain John Fay, of Louisburg and Crown Point memory, was of the committee appointed to make such an adjustment that all soldiers should receive a proportionate compensation for their services, whether longer or shorter, and "that the cost of the war might fall in just proportion upon the property of the town."* So scrupulously just and exact were these men, that persons who had moved into town after the war had began were only assessed their proportion according to the time of their arrival. And thus the early possessors of these fields added to their sublime heroism under arms the radiant grace of Christian justice and equality under the bowers of peace. At the close of seven years of blazing conflict, and when the glare of war subsided, they relumined their forest homes with the celestial light they had caught from the Gospel.

Justice to the inhabitants and to the truth of history requires an allusion to the relations which this town bore with the Shays' insurrection. It will be remembered that after the close of the war, in the midst of the sufferings which ensued from the dilapidation of the currency, Massachusetts manifested her fidelity to the confederation and her own character by adopting a manly and large policy of taxation. In some parts of the State, where the resources of the people were straitened, this necessity and sys-

—* Note Q.

tem of taxation was severely but unavoidably felt. The aggravations of suits and of executions issuing from the courts under the rigors of the old law practice, undoubtedly contributed additional provocation to the general discontent. Shays' rebellion in 1786 and 1787 was the consequence. It had a large support in the county of Worcester, and more especially in the northern towns. It is not necessary at this day to discuss the question how far that public situation should be pleaded in mitigation of the judgment of history; for no man in his senses now justifies that rebellion. It is clear, however, that a somewhat tolerant judgment was pronounced by the men of that time. A sufficient illustration of this may be found in the fact that to the Massachusetts Convention which assembled for the ratification of the Constitution of the United States, and which was held shortly after the dispersion of Shays' forces, there were sent from the county of Worcester a very large number of delegates who had been avowed and active insurgents. The adoption of the federal constitution in the state convention was only carried by a majority of nineteen votes, the delegation of our own county alone casting a large preponderance of votes against it; so large that if it had depended upon this ancient and historical Worcester, the constitution of glory and felicity to the millions past and to come in America, would have been refused by this colony, and, as I believe, would then have been rejected also by New York, and would have been lost forever, with what disastrous consequences to the races here and over the globe, it is not worth while now to speculate. After a somewhat careful study of the action of the county of Worcester, it is my conviction that the demoralization of Shays' rebellion was connected with her course in relation to the constitution; and it is a compensation, which goes far to relieve our present regret, to know that the poison of insubordination was checked before it became fatal. Kindly and justly may we drop the veil of oblivion over this exceptional chapter, since her record in the Revolution and in the recent war with treason is affluent and sublime with self-sacrifice and heroic deeds, of which the memory and the honor shall be immortal.

This town of Royalston was bordered on the southerly outline by a population which shared to a considerable extent in the sympathies of the movements of Shays. I should judge from its contiguites, as I also infer from slight and inexplicit entries in its records, that a large number of its own citizens accorded with the opinons prevaling in the adjacent communities. But after diligent search it has not happened to me to discern any evidence whatever, that a single man here joined bodily with the insurgents, or ever took up arms against his country or his country-men. Such is undoubtedly the fact of our local history. You know that the last bubble of Shays' burst in the midst of a January snow-storm, a little south of us, at Petersham, when his wretched adherents broke and scattered before the law through all this northern section. Some of their frightened numbers passed up along the valley of the Tully through West Royalston to the frontier of the state. I know from what I heard in my boyhood, that in their forlorn and panic-stricken passage through that section of the town they received the Christian hospitality of warm hearth-stones, and that only; of all which, for the sake of our common humanity, we ought not now greatly to complain.

This, truthfully told according to all the knowledge I have been able to acquire, is the part of your ancestors in a rebellion which rose and disappeared like a dream.

Our patriotic journal is as continuous as it is creditable. In the war with Great Britain in 1812—15, our fathers were alike "Federal" in politics and steadfast in their patriotism. They believed throughout in the policy of Hamilton, and Ames, and Strong, but they never stood away from the national colors. Accordingly they sent a fine, large company of Grenadiers for coast defence to Boston, under circumstances of departure which made the scene to be remembered as pathetic and impressive. Those men all returned without a casualty and nearly one half of their number live to day to celebrate their federal and bloodless campaign. Other citizens of the town, however, went out into the active service and mingled in the engagements of that war on distant fields.*

In the late war with the Rebellion the conduct of this town has been such as I am proud to record. Her people stood early and constant by the government, and by the principle of universal liberty. In the defence of them they have strained every energy under circumstances of embarrassment not shared by many other sections of the state. The opening conflict found the place considerably exhausted of its young men, whom more exciting fields of enterprise had drawn away from their hill-sides, and the second year of the struggle greatly increased that exhaustion. But still upward and onward to the last victories our people answered to the calls of the country, filled their quotas and never fell below the example of their Revolutionary sires. Several of the

—*Note R.

native-born sons of Royalston have been promoted as general officers to high commands in the national army. When I consider that the population has been declining within the last decade, and that this decline represents chiefly the departure of those who are within the age of military requisition, I confess my surprise and admiration over the roll of those who have borne the name of our birth-place on the many fields of this war. The great cost to the manhood of the Union in defence of its life becomes solemn to our senses when we examine in detail the account of the several towns of Massachusetts. From this little community alone ONE HUNDRED AND TEN men have enlisted in the sublime work of saving their country by arms. Of this enlistment an uncommon proportion have fallen to their last sleep. In the deadly night-shades of Carolina, in the early battles which cheered every loyal heart by the tidings wafted from Roanoke and Newbern, in the conflict with an armed foe and with a more fatal climate on the lower Mississippi, in the terrible and unavailing slaughter at Drury's Bluff and Cold Harbor, on guard and in the trenches and along the blazing lines whenever and wherever they were called, in Libby, which is yet unavenged, in the stockade of Andersonville, from which the voices of thirty thousand Union boys, starved, tortured, murdered, now break the silence of death in a chorus-cry for justice. The soldiers of Royalston have lifted their souls to the contemplation of duty and to the heights of courage, have offered up their lives to the sudden death of the field, and the slow death of the prison, and have perpetuated the name of the town which enrolled them in annals of immortal lustre. So long as we and our children shall enjoy the blessings of Union which they died to save, and shall bless the God of our ancestors for sealing with their sacrifices the freedom of all races in America, their names shall be cherished by us and shall descend to everlasting remembrance. Let those names, every one of them, be attached to this commemorative address, and be engrossed in your official records for endurance till these hills shall melt away. Ye gallant survivors, welcome to day! Ye gallant dead, hail and farewell!*

Public action here in relation to the interests of Education† has been so like that of other Massachusetts towns that the meagre record scarcely requires transcribing or analyzing. Popular education, in this class of municipal corporations remote from the sea-board, was of necessity considerably neglected until the close of the Revolutionary war. Subsistence for natural life takes precedence of intellectual culture. And yet, at the first beginning the thought of "schooling" cropped out among the demonstrative movements of the settlers. A glimmer of it appeared in 1769, when three pounds were appropriated to this object. The first school-house was erected on the North Easterly line of this public common, not by general taxation, but by a vote of the town authorizing individuals to make such use of its land. The hand of Joseph Lee, graduate of Harvard College, appears evident in this first offical act for the cause of the modern age. After the close of the war, in 1786, the lot of land which had been set apart for schools by the first proprietors, and which had been leased out down to that day, was sold, and the proceeds of that sale are the foundation of your present school fund. In 1790 the first school committee was chosen. In 1791 a military nomenclature for schools was superceded by a better.

*Note S.
†Note T.

and the division of the town into educational "squadrons" was exchanged for a distribution into school "Districts." In 1792 for the first time a special town meeting was called and held for the purpose of adapting the high business of schooling to the established laws and policy of the Commonwealth. Then were commenced the signal measures for educating the rising generation of an augmented population to the future exigencies of a sovereign Commonwealth and of the newly established American gorvernment. In 1798 the town first voted to erect schoolhouses in the several districts, out of which vote have risen the more commodious temples of the present day within which are enshrined the best hopes of our earthly strength and our eternal life. The progress of years has brought with it the progress of enlarged ideas and of enlarged expenditures for education until now, in addition to the old school fund whose increments have swelled the principal to the sum of fifteen hundred dollars, and in addition to the special fund of five thousand dollars bequeathed for this purpose by the late Rufus Bullock, the town votes respectable annual appropriations which, let us believe, are to be still further increased till the youth born and reared here shall be attracted by moral incitements to remain and abide to adorn the homes of their fathers with the glories of a more elevated social life.

Of the teachers of schools in this place, many of whom afterwards became eminent on other fields of life, my personal recollection selects Mr. Thomas J. Lee, son of that first revered minister and author of the spelling book which was used in my childhood. Over the interval of forty years his spare form, his gentle manners, his suavity, his dignity, rise before me and command the respect of memory, as then they commanded the obedient veneration of a child.

Providence has not brought our growth to this day exempt from the mortal lot of occasional years of silent and solemn drama. Even here, where salubrity is the normal rule, death at times has held the high carnival. In 1772, ten years after the first settlement, the population was almost literally decimated by the death of fifty-two persons in the sweep of one of the epidemics which have not been uncommon in New England. In 1795 a throat disease, and other sicknesses, carried away eighty-six souls from the habitations of the living,—whole groups of children from the same roof,—six persons passing through the swelling flood in a single day. The like of this, however, has been witnessed elsewhere, and our dispensations have not distinguished us from the providences of God in other localities. And yet for those exceptional days of mourning and of darkness the many other years have brought the grand average of their compensation. In the long duration of time the heavens and the earth are in your favor. Here the skies are always northern, and the constellations through the marches of the night shine brightly, and the elastic air from the mountains beyond continually alights at your doors and windows to whisper to the arm-chair and bed-side within the patriarchal assurance of longevity. Nothing better outside of Newport, Rhode Island, where it has seemed to me that every body lives to be old, has crossed my reading. One of your committee has placed in my hands a list of the preserved names of ninety-four individuals who have deceased here above the age of eighty and below the age of one-hundred and five* years of life. And this is only a part of them
—*Note U.

all. I ought to add that the only one who reached this last named ultimatum was good old Mrs. Susannah Carpenter, whose kinswomen live among you to day,—who was so far back of your forefathers that it was her son who came here as one of the early settlers, whose lot she followed into this hopeful wilderness,—who in the blindness of old age was carried by her lively grandchildren out to tea among the neighbors, that always invited her to bring with her the tea-set which she had inherited from her first husband, a sailor,—and the best of china it was, as also the first in the town, relics of which are still preserved by her descendants. Old age in Royalston is as natural as it is scriptural. You, Reverend pastors, may safely preach it among the promises,—only not forgetting to recommend the kind of living that leads to it.

My recollections of this town, going back thirty, forty years, draw before me its scenes of life, action, and responsibility as when quite young I witnessed them in the hands of the generation then moving on the stage. Here was then in the true sense a rural life. The water power on Miller's river and the other streams had not to a great extent been improved for the various manufactures which now so largely supply and stimulate your resources. A simple, prosperous, contented agriculture for the most part engaged the people. The hand loom was in many a household, and under the æolian cadence of the spinning wheel I remember myself to have passed in early evening to the sweet sleep of childhood. The arrival from Boston, seventy miles, of the teams of Piper and the two Pierces, afterwards kept up by Whitney, and the unlading of their freight at the store doors of Estabrook and Bullock and Gregory, imparted incident and excitement for the public curiosity. The exchange between this agriculture and the trade of the sea-board was regular and wholesome. I am bound to allow that the March-meetings in those days were a little jolly, but there may have been some virtues to atone which were more predominant then, than they are now. Once a week our portly fellow citizen of that time, Jonathan Pierce drove the post and carried the mail between Worcester and Keene through Royalston, bringing to us the weekly papers, the regular politics, the more distant gossip, and helping us along generally in our conformity with the outside world. This mission, commencing about the year 1800, he performed nearly a quarter of a century; and happy days they were.

From this I might easily diverge to speak of the prominent men whom I learned so greatly to respect as sources of radiating influence from this central common. The minister, Mr. Perkins, of grave yet pleasant memory,—how I remember him, in his long floating, summer *toga*, driving us in at the eight o'clock bell on every Saturday evening; Esquire Joseph Estabrook, our first post-master, our first gentleman, our first senator, to my perceptions blending the old and the new school of manners, who began as a trader and adopted in later years the pleasant vocation of a grazier, having a genius for noble cattle as quick and intuitive as Daniel Webster ever possessed, whose blood, whether remaining here or transferred in honorable connections to other places, honors the parent stock; Dr. Batcheller, absolutely august in his proportions, always riding rapidly and smoking as fast, with a short, genial nod and a happy word for everybody and especially for the young of both sexes; Maj. Gen. Franklin Gregory, who succeeded to Estabrook on the other side of the street, gentleman by nature, taking by instinct to the military in which he excelled all others and in that capacity presided at one of the festive boards in reception of Lafayette, the most enterprising merchant this town ever had, and inaugurating here her largest trade, whose untimely death in 1836 at 44 was a public loss irreparable; and one other, who far outlived all these his associates, whom as exemplar of a long, simple, successful, and virtuous life, whom as many times your representative, twice your Senator, your delegate to the Constitutional Conventions of 1820 and 1852, your honored townsman in his life time, and benefactor in death, I should proudly describe, but that the inheritance of his name forbids;—these, and others, challenge my memories in this hour and hallow the spot of a youthful love. They have all gone, and with most of their day and generation they repose in these burial grounds and almost in our presence. And so on this occasion the past comes back to me in the memorials which are treasured but fractured, leaving to me this morning the melancholy pleasure of uniting my heart with the friends that survive.

The industrial characteristics of the town have changed with the exigencies of the age. The water-falls have been reclaimed, and the ever varying arts and industries inaugurated by the use of steam as a practical agency and by the division of labor have come in here as elsewhere and have somewhat transformed that which was formerly a rural life. There was very early in its history a quite respectable use of woolen machinery*, which under the new dispensation of industry has been greatly increased, until no small part of the local market for consumption and val-

—*Note V.

ues is now found in the wheels, and cogs, and spindles, which make South Royalston the central point of active enterprise and production. While that busy hive on your Southerly border, having the double advantage of the River and the Rail Road, must henceforth maintain its supremacy, let us indulge the hope that only fraternal relations shall subsist between the sections, and that all together will continue for generations to be contented and united under the patriarchal banner.

To the agricultural identities of the population I mainly ascribe its almost stationary numerical peculiarity. From 1790 to 1860, a term of seventy years, the number of inhabitants only varied from 1,130 to 1,486, from one decade to another sometimes gaining a little and sometimes losing nearly the same. You will observe in the returns of the census perhaps quite enough of the evidence of this kind of stability. Those returns range as follows:

1790	1800	1810	1820	1830	1840	1850	1860
1,130	1,243	1,415	1,424	1,493	1,667	1,546	1,486

But this character is not the worst that can happen to a town. If it will maintain its virtue, its power and beneficence shall rise superior even above the loss of numbers.

But there is a better proof of the moral and productive forces of the residents in the statistics of valuation which are forwarded from the State House; for they demonstrate that a youthful vigor still abides in the ancient town, and that its progress is still onward and upward. Study them and take the courage of faith and hope.

1790,	£1,622, 6s, 1 1-4d,	Amount
1800,	$8,656 51	of
1810,	10,621 67	
1820,	13,480 02	Income.
1830,	$340,598 00	Valuation
1840,	433,314 43	of
1850,	751,008 00	
1860,	822,257 00	Estates.

From these statements it appears that the valuation of the property of your population,—and I believe that estates have at no time been over-estimated here,—has since 1790, the year of the first returns, been constantly and rapidly increasing. In twenty years, from 1840 to 1860, it has quite nearly doubled. This I regard as most hopeful and encouraging.

Your annals are not of the prizes of fortune and affluence, nor contain they any modern chapter of poverty. Those annals tell us of systematic toil, and patriotic struggle, and patient endurance, and the christian faith. The economics of industry and the riches of the heart are the pride and solace of the record. This town should never be forgotten by her sons wheresoever they may wander. For myself, as here the first breath was drawn, so here the last word should willingly be uttered. If the sons and daughters could abandon and forget her in pursuit of more exciting scenes, even in larger numbers than they have yet gone,—if the country simplicity of the early days should settle down like the clouds of the Province over her fields and her farms, my last remembrance should still revert to the happy hills and pastures of childhood and I would still address her in the language of mingled encouragement and admonition, worthy of the poet of the DESERTED VILLAGE:

> "Aid slighted truth with thy persuasive strain;
> Teach erring man to spare the rage of gain;
> Teach him, that towns of native strength possest,
> Though very poor, may still be very blest;
> That trade's proud empire hastes to swift decay,
> As ocean sweeps the labour'd mole away;
> While self-dependant power can time defy,
> As rocks resist the billows of the sky."

Friends and fellow citizens, this imperfect tribute to the qualities and the labors of our ancestors must be brought to a close. At the end of one hundred years, we, their descendants, have assembled to contemplate in brief review their lives and achievements. I submit it to impartial judgment, that their conduct in the early settlement, in the management of the town, in the cultivation of the fields, in their relations with the great events of the country, in all the duties of church and state, in the salutary examples which have passed from one generation to another,—in religion, industry, politics, and daily life,—has been such that we may rehearse it with pride and commend it to those who shall come after us. This congregation of the living is equalled in numbers by those who sleep in this town in the quiet enclosures of the dead.* They speak to us out of their silence and repeat the lesson of their lives. As they were bound together by the ties of friendship in the primitive period of their trials, and have kept the counsels of peace and unity through all the stages of this history, so let that spirit control another age and the felicities of social life go hand in hand with public stability and prosperity. As they adapted themselves to the changing

—*Note W.

requisitions of the general industry and economy, so let the tides of occupation, as they come and go with you, bear onward a community never behind but always advancing. As they never failed to uphold the honor of their country by their hearts, by their declarations, and by their arms, so let the American Union and the Commonwealth of Massachusetts find in this town forever most constant friends and most gallant defenders. As they have transmitted to our keeping the institutions of worship and education, by them at all times well endowed and well supported, so let the endowments be multiplied and the support be enlarged till the bells of the churches and the schools shall sound a welcome in every ear. And when, after the passage of another century, your successors shall meet over your dust to celebrate their day, may it be the happiness of the intervening generations to have provided for them as little for reproach and as much for devout thanksgiving as we ourselves have received from our fathers.

MEMORIALS AND GARLANDS.

A POEM

DELIVERED AT THE ROYALSTON CENTENNIAL, AUGUST 23, 1865.

BY ALBERT BRYANT, A. M.

He who, led by childhood's memories, to his early home returns,
Oft will find there naught familiar save the names on funeral urns.
Scenes and faces, loved and longed for, left behind in time's swift track,
Airy nothings are, that vanish, which no pilgrimage brings back.
But the hills and streams are constant, for his tears they make amends:
Them he greets with exultation and communes with them as friends.

Old Monadnock! o'er thy summit though the mists forever drift,
And around thee in the drama fickle scenes and actors shift,
All the centuries in their process cannot change thy green and gray,
And in morning light resplendent *thine* our welcome is to-day.

We have seen, when winter rages, thy cold forehead awe the vale,
Heard the brooks like bells of silver round thy skirts bid spring-time hail.
Welcomed cooling showers of summer when o'er thee the clouds are rolled,
And rejoiced when Autumn clad thee in her crimson, green and gold.
Count the hundred years, Monadnock, and how many festal throngs
Climb again thy rugged shoulders! they are silent like their songs.
At thy feet to-day we gather, when the conflict round us rolls,
Let thy strength with courage gird us and thy patience calm our souls!

From our western borders —Listen! and below the vale of mills,
Noisy water-falls are joining in the welcome of the hills.
From the gorge beneath the shadows, throned upon the granite rocks,
Shouts to us the Royal Cascade, tossing loose her shining locks.
"Hail! to-day, ye sons and daughters of the household! welcome home!
Time has changed you,— thinned your numbers since you left my forest dome.
Centuries bury all the living, fill the valley, bow the hill,
But they never reach the waters, ever changing, changeless still."
And the Southern cascades answer, hurrying in their triple fall—
"Hail! to-day, ye sons and daughters of the household! welcome all!"

Torrents! back we send your greetings! hear our swiftly throng-
ing feet,
Like the rush of many waters sounding through the village street.
From the study, desk, and counter, from the work-shops and the
fields,
This illustrious morning leads us forth to harvests memory yields,
And these once familiar voices fall like music on our ears,
While we bind in golden bundles all the old town's hundred
years.

Let us break to-day the silence where the ancient forest waves,
And the choicest garlands scatter on our fathers' fading graves.
Victors in the dreary woodland, fields and orchards were their
spoils,
Now, and ever, green and fruitful by their patience and their toils.
Their's the hands that set the roof-trees under which your chil-
dren play,
Shades they yield that live forever, though the fostering hands
are clay.
When your sons go forth with honor from these hills to serve or
rule,
Bless the wisdom of the fathers, founders of the village school.
When o'er vale and hill are swelling the clear tones of Sabbath
bells,
Of the churches' pious founders half the sacred music tells;
And grey men for little children as they gather at the knee,
While they tell with tears of gladness, how our glorious land is
free,
Backward trace the thrilling story till they reach the crimson
sod,

Where old heroes wrote with sword-blades that no lord is king,
   —but God!
By the northern lakes and forests where they dared the wintry
   sleet;
By the Delaware's broad waters where they passed with bleed-
   ing feet;
Down the Carolinean river, bound by one red battle plain,
We again behold them marching, oh! they have not marched
   in vain.
Here beneath the forest shadows, though our fathers' ashes sleep,
Jealous vigils for their children their stern spirits ever keep.
And from every startled fireside, when the battle call goes by,
Muster they the sons of freemen forth again to win and die.

   To the grave yard come, below the hill,
   When the cares of busy day are still,
   And spell from broken stones the names
   That kindled Freedom's holy flames.
   The dewy pines a hundred years,
   Have wet the ancient mounds with tears.

   Though breaking day its splendor weaves
   Along a million pointed leaves,
   Or moon-beams o'er the solemn wood
   At evening draw their shining hood,
   No light, at morn or evening, shines
   Upon the graves beneath the pines.

   When long ago these graves were made,
   No forest roots disturbed the spade,
   Nor shadows on the coffins fell,

Save such as mourner's tears can tell.
But since Death called the ground his own,
These ranks of giant trees have grown.

The stalk our fathers died to rear,
As grandly branches far and near,
Its roots are wrapped about their bones,
They speak in all its wind-stirred tones,
Nor shall their graves forgotten be
'Neath Liberty's immortal tree!

To the grave yard, then, below the hill
Come when the cares of day are still;
And trace on living stones the names
That kindled Freedom's holy flames;
The dewy pines, a hundred years,
Have wet these ancient mounds with tears.

As old age, its youth recalling, overleaps what lies between,
So the far off past we honor, honoring most the dimly seen,
But while lingering with the fathers, whose great acts built up the state,
All the Century's thronging stories for our humble garlands wait.
On this birth-day you remember what has made the old town dear,
And has traced her name the brighter with each fleet, increasing year.
You remember the old School House where you gathered, long ago,

Spurning with bare feet the hill-side, toiling muffled through the snow;
The long seats, where little urchins, with their toes stretched toward the floor,
Leaning on the desks their elbows, hummed the lessons o'er and o'er.
The huge fire of logs in winter, thawing all the nearer rows,
While, beside the airy windows, the tall back seats shook and froze.
The school-masters and their ferules, dreadful to the rogue and dunce,
But with praise and long recesses for the good—as you were once.
Some were full of college wisdom and of frolic free of harm,
Some taught school in winter only, in the summer tilled the farm.
O these masters and their ferules! they are dust like common dust,
Long ago our tears fell o'er them, they have passed on high we trust.

You remember youths and maidens whose dear voices never tire,
At the merry singing meetings to instruct the village choir.
The old leaders with their pitch-pipes, till *he* woke the viol string,
Whose memorial is with us—" He taught children how to sing."

Some the meeting-house remember at the joining of the streets,
With the Gabriel o'er the pulpit, and square pews with slamming seats.
There our fathers held town meetings in their democratic way,

And on Sundays, with their households, heard the pastor preach
and pray.
Later days brought in new notions; then arose the modern spire.
But the clanging bell fell with it, telling tales of midnight fire.
And when, by the distant farm-house, lay at morn a half burned
leaf
Of the ancient pulpit Bible, all eyes there were wet with grief.
Grave and solemn was the pastor in his quaint cocked hat and
gown,
And at door-ways careful parents, when they saw him riding
down,
In the days e'er graceful reverence from New England youth had
fled,
Placed their children, with clean faces, to bow low each curly
head.
One pale browed and gentle preacher some of us cannot forget,
On the Sea of Glass now singing, where the wild waves never
fret.
To the tree of life he led us, underneath its healing leaves,
And his farewell smile goes with us till we come with many
sheaves.

Could we fix upon the canvas all the throng that jostles past,
What strange scenes the motley faces of a hundred years would
cast!
By the mourner's tear stained visage, by each heart felt smile or
frown,
In the oddest contradiction smirks the buffoon or the clown.
'Tis the curious and unusual that remain for after times;
While the worthiest want a record, we immortalize Old Grimes.

Full of pranks and jovial fancies which our fathers hardly bore,
He still walks in fire-side story, in that long, blue coat he wore.
And beside him wanders, love-lorn, with the ballad's quaint sad tones,
Moving our grandmother's pity, the poor lover, Crazy Jones.

" Ho time is a Goblin, and awful the dance
Whose mazes return not, but always advance,
 Through which his gay partners he gleefully whirls,
 And to bald shrivelled crones turns the fairest of girls."
So laughed the strange teller of fortunes, Old Nance.

She dwelt in a valley far over the hill,
Her two eyes were piercing, her accents were shrill,
 Through her town and our town wandered her fame,
 Till the sage and the simple, and all ages came,
To learn of the Future: five dimes was the bill.

One day in December the school master sat
By her wide chimney corner spell-bound by her chat,
 As she told how a widow with plenty of gold,
 With houses, and acres, and beauties untold,
Would be his for the asking—with never a brat.

Now fleeter and fleeter the swift moments flew,
The chimney was wide, and fierce the wind blew,
 The smoke and the ashes drew out and drew in,
 And the school master fancied the dame was so thin,
That he saw, for a moment, the fire light shine through.

The master was eager, the dame's tongue was brisk,
His fortune grew larger—and lesser the risk,

>Till his locks rose upright and he screamed, to behold
>>Old Nancy together like burnt paper rolled,
And up the vast flue disappear with a whisk.

By the chimney still stands an empty arm chair,
To attest that my story is truthful and fair,
>>What became of the master I never have known,
>>And, for aught I can tell, the merry old crone
Is completing his fortunes up in the air.

There are customs of our fathers, pleasant, passing out of mind
Round which, on this day of memory, we memorial ivy bind.
How the apple bees in autumn make the farm-house kitchen ring,
As the merry swains and maidens pare the fruit, and cut, and string,
When the pumpkin pies were eaten, and the cider pitcher drained
And the girls were home attended, oh! what troubled dreams remained!
In the plough-boy's haunted slumbers, came again the bright eyed groups,
With their pans of well strung quarters binding him in long damp loops.

Then the Huskings in October, when the old barn floor appears
Jubilant with corn in bundles, and the heaps of shining ears.
O'er the dimly lighted rafters the queer imp of frolic walks,
And the laughter of the huskers drowns the rustling of the stalks.

After Harvesting was over, came, and still will come the day,
When the house is set in order, and the work is laid away;
And the old folks at the firesides, in their newest coat and gown,

Welcome home to spend Thanksgiving, all the children of the town.

Often when the snows were level, and young hearts were free of care,
Came the sleigh rides in the moon-light of the frosty winter air,
Like the music of the sleigh-bells, to the happy youth who ride,
Are the voices of the present, loudly, ceaselessly beside,
Like the music of those sleigh-bells, swelling, dying, gone at last,
All the years and all their treasures hurry to the voiceless past.
Yet each year's remembered music, adds new notes to rouse or calm,
And the golden year draws nearer, with the Century's finished Psalm.

Though we see not the world moving, how it flies beneath the sun;
By our reckoning—oh! *they* count not where the thousand years are one.
E'en the Century leaves behind it deeds of progress grandly wrought,
And makes hallowed ground forever of the fields our age has fought.
Our old town has seen the dawning of the glorious latter days,
Her slain heroes are not silent in the earth's wide Hymn of Praise.
But not *mine* to weave the garland who still hear their well kept vows;
There are crowns of loftier splendor for their beautiful, dear brows,

Radiant upon the foreheads of a hundred thousand bold,
On the sea of battle drifted, in the graves of Honor cold.
And not mine to say "they conquered," O! their victory's rare reward,
Hear the millions they delivered tell the story to the Lord!

Our memorial song is ended, our memorial day soon done;
Soon amid the falling shadows we and it shall journey on.
On the troubled sea before us, all our hopes and all our fears,
We again go down to venture for another hundred years.
You, sir, at whose potent summons the charmed years before us stand,
Here the call to higher stations in the state and in the land.
Some will find distinguished places, some will seek a shaded spot;
Which they find but little matters so they labor in their lot.

Farewell mountains, hills and waters, like the vapors ye must fade;
We shall come again,—one morning, when all history is made.
We shall see the roll of honor, 'tis for crowns and kingdoms won'
When the Lord of all the Centuries tells His Little Ones "Well done."

APPENDIX.

NOTE A—PAGE 21.   OUR BIRTHDAY.

The incorporate life of Royalston began with its charter, February 16th, 1765. But a Centennial celebration on these hights in the depth of winter was not to be thought of. The circumstances indicated a "movable," rather than an "immovable" festival. Accordingly, the commemoration of the hundredth anniversary of our Birthday was deferred till August,—a month in which elevated localities, mountain air, and green hillsides are in request, and near the close of which there is usually an interval of comparative leisure, favorable to the entertainment and enjoyment of friends, and the season more commonly chosen by our absent ones for revisiting their old friends and homes.

NOTE B—PAGES 26 AND 27.   TITLES, TERRITORY AND PROPRIETORS.

The unappropriated lands of the Province were disposed of by the General Court, from time to time, either by private Grants, or public Sales; not so much, it would seem, for immediate income, as for the encouragement of settlement, and to maintain a liberal policy toward the citizens.

Grants were usually made upon petitions, setting forth some special public service or hardship. The successful applicant located his land in some specified territory, and returned a *plat* thereof, taken by "a Surveyor and Chairman under oath," to the Court for confirmation. The Record of these doings, in the Secretary's Office, constituted the *Title* of the grantee.

Sales were ordered by the General Court, and conducted by a special joint committee, instructed as to the terms of the sale, and empowered to convey the same, giving deeds and taking bonds. These conveyances, or indentures, entered with the Deeds and Records for the county within which the land was situated, constituted the *Title* of the purchaser.

Our territory passed from public to private hands by both of these methods; four private grants having been located and confirmed prior to the public sale of the residue, in 1752. This sale was conducted by a joint committee, consisting of John Chandler, and James Minor of the Council, and Mr. Speaker, (Thomas Hubbard,) John Tyng and William Lawrence of the House. It took place Dec. 21st, 1752; conveyance was made on the 27th; and the indenture was recorded with the Deeds and Records for the county of Worcester, Jan. 1st, of the following year, in Book 32, pages 123, 124, 125, and 126. An attested copy of the document occupies the first pages of a copy of the Proprietors' Records in the custody of our Town Clerk.

And thus we have the *Titles* of the land, whether as held by grantees, or purchasers.

The Territory is ascertained from these Titles; from whence it appears that the four grants comprised 2.300 acres; and the purchase 28.357 acres. The subsequent questions and investigations, as between the purchasers and the General Court, show that these figures were not too high; but rather that they fell short of expressing our territory, as it stood when the town was incorporated. The excisions and annexations since have somewhat curtailed the number of our acres, but precisely how much can only be determined by surveys based upon the several "Acts" by which these changes have been effected. The town valuation of 1864, reports 26.882 acres.

The original *Proprietors* of these lands can be but imperfectly illustrated.

One "*Pierpont* and others," held the largest Grant; but who they were, and why they received this Province land, we have been unable to ascertain. Their land is laid down on the *Plan* of *the Proprietors*, [the title of the purchasers as distinguished from the grantees,] nearly in the north-east corner of the town, as now bounded. It must have nearly, or quite, covered the farms of John Wood, Joel and Daniel Taft, Capt. Wm. Chase, Joel Howard, Jocob Hale, John Holman, Wm. Withington and Nathan Reed,—we give the names as laid down on the Map of Royalston, taken in 1831.

Joseph Priest's grant is also laid down distinctly on said Plan, immediately east of Pierpont's, and on both sides of the brook bearing his name, covering, it would seem the Bemis farms, and other small places, north and south of the same.

The grant next east, and taking up all our territory to Winchendon line, belonged to one Thomas Hapgood of Marlboro.

The Honorable Secretary of the Commonwealth has furnshed a copy of the doings of the General Court, illustrating this grant. It was ordered in 1742, in "consideration of services in the war with the eastern Indians and his sufferings by reason of wounds received from them, whereby in his advanced age he was disabled from labor for the support of himself and family."

Documents from the same source give us the names of the grantees, and the date of the grant, situated at the west part of the town. This grant was made, Dec. 15th, 1737, to Benoni Moore, Joseph Pettey, and Robert Cooper. Before 1765, however, it had passed into the hands of Samuel Hunt of Northfield, and others. The terms of the grant, as ascertained by Benoni Peck, Esq. located the same between what is now Athol. and the Province line—'to be laid out 480 rods long on the eastern line of what is now Warwick, and 200 rods wide from west to east, and no more.' He also satisfied himself that the grant was made in consideration of services, rendered by the grantees, in burying the bleached bones of certain soldiers, who, led by Capt. Beers, were marching from the river below to the assistance of Northfield, but fell into an ambuscade and were slaughtered by the Indians. A hill, which Mr. Peck has visited, situated near Northfield, still bears the name of the unfortunate Captain.

The names of the *purchasers*, were Samuel Watts, Thomas Hubbard, (then speaker of the House,) Isaac Freeman, Joseph Richards, Isaac Royal, Caleb Dana, James Otis, Joseph Wilder Jr. and John Chandler Jr. The names of Freeman and Richards, soon disappear from the Records, and in their place we have those of the Honorable Thomas Hancock and John Erving, Esq. The former died in 1764, and his nephew, John Hancock, whom he educated, and who succeeded to his large fortune and extensive mercantile business, became one of the Proprietors.

Samuel Watts Esq. was of Chelsea, stood at the head of the Proprietors, moderated their first meetings, and was active in settling this town; but otherwise we gather nothing respecting him.

Thomas Hubbard was long a prominent Boston man, often in public stations. He was *treasurer* of the Propriety till his death in 1773.

Isaac Royal, who has given us his name, aided in establishing the preached Gospel among us, and who remembered his namesake in his will, is mentioned honorably at pps. 30, 31, of the Address. We received our name from him before he contracted the *taint* of Toryism; and the facts, recited by Mr. Bullock, taken in connection with the other fact, that he made provision for the law professorship, gave one of his 200 acre lots, for the benefit of our schools, together with numerous other liberal bequests for public purposes in this country, by *his last will and testament,* executed in England, and while under the ban of outlawry, may surely justify so far as he is concerned, our continued love of our old name. His penitence came too late for his comfort; but it came so strong, and under such circumstances, as should redeem his name from too severe reproach.

Caleb Dana Esq. of Cambridge and *Capt. Joseph Wilder* of Lancaster were among the *working* men of the Proprietors. Their names appear on the committees that had much to do, personally, in bringing forward the settlement of the territory. At a later period the captain seems to have come hither for a wife. We find the following Record among the marriages by Rev. Mr. Lee, "Nov. 14th, 1782. Capt. Joseph Wilder of Lancaster, and Mrs. Hepzibah Norton were married."

John Erving Esq. besides his interest in this territory, was a large purchaser and proprietor of other public lands; and, like Isaac Royal, he gave his name to a township south-west of us.

Col. *John Chandler*, was a Worcester man,—the third of the same given and surname, who held, in succession, the office of Judge of Probate for our County. And a genial Judge he must have been, " keeping open doors on court days, and spreading his tables for the entertainment of all suitors in his court." Truly, if his justice and mercy were equal to his hospitality, the widow's heart must have sung for joy under his administration. Of him and his ancestry honorable mention is made in the annals of his early home. Both his and his father's name appear in the sale and on the title deed of this town. He, too, in those times that tried the souls of men, went with the Tories, left his country and was outlawed; but not till he had planted a seed that flowed on in the channels of patriotism. George Bancroft (now laboring upon our national history) is his grandson; and the wife of the honored and venerable Ex. Gov. Lincoln, his granddaughter. Let his early and better life, and his eminently American descendants, veil the grand mistake of his Revolutionary politics.

But if it be ungrateful to reflect that these two prominent Proprietors went with the king and parliament against the country, it is a matter of satisfaction that two of far greater worth stood at the front of the rightful and winning party,—James Otis, the fine scholar, distinguished advocate and dauntless patriot, a son of flame as well as of thunder, bearing down upon the royal cause with fiery rhetoric and resistless argument, and *John Hancock*, early winning from Gov. Gage the opinion, that his " offences against the king were of so flagitious a nature as to admit of no other consideration than that of condign punishment." an opinion which he also entertained with respect to Samuel Adams.

But the record of such men needs no recital of ours. James Otis was the *orator* of those days. John Hancock did not often attempt a speech; but his weight of character, his wisdom, his talents as a business man, and as a presiding and executive officer, and the dignity and power of his presence, made him great. The first to sign the Declaration of Independence, the stroke of his pen impressed upon that immortal document something of that nobility and grandeur which belonged both to his character and his life.

During the Revolution the business of settling this town was greatly retarded; and there are no records of Proprietors' meetings. Upon the return of more favorable days, the Proprietors resumed their labors; and we find several new names superseding those of the old. We only recite them. Samuel A. Otis, Benjamin Kent, John Erving 3d, William Haskins, Willis Hall, Cotton Tufts, and Dr. Samuel Danforth.

NOTE C—PAGE 29.   SCENERY, &C.

Few towns can boast greater, or more interesting Natural Scenery than Royalston. High and rugged hills, noble swells of excellent land, and intersecting vallies, make up the general *contour*. Overlooking the surrounding country by its general elevation, it has also commanding eminences from which the eye takes in wider sweeps of vision, while it looks down on nearer objects of interest,—the clustering hamlets, and isolated farmhouses, the orchards, groves and woodlands, the shimmering ponds, and the meandering water-courses. From several of these eminences both the Monadnock and the Wachusett stand out in bold relief. Our horizon is bounded on the east and north-east by the high hills in Ashburnham, Rindge and New Ipswich, and on the west and north-west by the distant Green mountain range. Among the points affording extended and beautiful prospects may be mentioned Fry's hill, north of the common, the highlands west of the north road leading to Fitzwilliam, sometimes called the *Back Bone* of Royalston, the south pasture on the farm of Mr. John Pierce, overlooking So. Royalston, and Jacob's hill, as the road from the centre turns abruptly to the north. The view from this last point is very fine. It looks out westwardly upon Long Pond, Tully river and another smaller stream, both of which come down from the wooded lands to the north, and run tortuously through the meadows at your feet into Long Pond. In front of you, and beyond the meadows and pond, the country rises rapidly, with broken face, to the west and north till it meets the line of the horizon. It is a lovely landscape, whether in Spring, Summer or Autumn; but splendid when the tints of the latter season are out in their glory; so great is the variety of foliage, so artistic the blending of the many hues, and so grand the amphitheater in which the whole is displayed. Sometimes, too, when the winter is coronated, and copse and woodland pendant with crystal ice, and the sun flashing upon it all, the scene is truly magnificent.

Of the gorges and waterfalls in Royalston, Professor Hitchcock, in his Geology of Massachusetts, pages 283 : 284. writes as follows ;—

"There are at least three waterfalls connected with deep gorges in Royalston, that are well worth the attention of those who are fond of wild natural scenery. About a mile west of the meeting-house and center of the town, is a deep valley running north and south, nearly across the town. Near the meeting-house is a pond which empties itself into this valley by plunging rapidly down a steep declivity, which must be 800 or 1000 feet high. It then empties into another large pond, or rather a remarkable expansion of a small tributary of Miller's river. At one part of the descent of the brook above named, it falls at least 200 feet by several leaps within a distance of a few rods, forming several very beautiful cascades. There the original forests have not been disturbed. The trees overhang the murmuring waters, half concealing the stream, while broken trees are plunged across it in all directions.

In the extreme north-west part of the town, on the farm of Calvin Forbes, a gorge and cascade exist of still greater interest; one of the finest indeed in the state. The stream is not more than 10 feet wide at the spot, but it descends 45 feet at a single leap into a large basin, which from its top has been excavated by the erosion of the waters. The sides, to the height of 50 or 60 feet, are formed of solid rocks; now retreating and now projecting: crowned at the summit with trees. Many of these lean over the gulf, or have fallen across it; so that upon the whole, the scene is one of great wildness and interest. * * *
It certainly deserves a name; and until a better one shall be proposed, I would suggest that of *The Royal Cascade*; partly in reference to the name of the town in which it is situated, and partly in reference to its *royal* character.

Two miles south of Royalston Center, on the road leading to Athol, is another cascade on a larger stream. Its width, indeed, must be as much at 25 feet, and its depth considerable. In a short distance here the water descends, at several successive leaps, as much as 200 feet, between high walls of gneiss and granite. Toward the upper part of the descent, several mills are erected; but a small part only of the water power is employed. Below the mills the stream passes into the woods; and toward the lowest part of the descent, we get a single view of two falls of about 25 feet each. * * * There is more of beauty and less of wildness at this spot than at the Royal Cascade. This stream also has been, and still more extensively can be, applied to useful purposes. Perhaps therefore, considering the character of our political institutions, and our well known reputation for utilitarian tendencies, this, rather in contrast to the Royal cascade, may be denominated *The Republican Cascade*. But if I can induce persons of taste and leisure to visit it, I care but little for the name."

In the early years, this town had a reputation for the productiveness of the soil, and the thrift of its agricultural population. A considerable surplus of corn, rye, barley, oats, hay and potatoes, was annually marketed abroad. Fine stock and good daries enriched the town and attracted trade. Now, however, neither the tillage nor the pastures, taken as a whole, yield as aforetimes, though there are still farms that make good crops, and pastures that turn out good cattle; enough to show that the fault is not altogether in the soil. In this, as in other towns, resolute and intelligent farmers make shining farms, and flourish in their honorable occupation. But the popular current is not in that direction, and in consequence not a little of our land is given over to "saplings." These, especially the pines, make rapid growth and are esteemed a good investment.

Our winters are long and the seasons come forward slowly; but then we are less liable to untimely frosts and severe droughts, and often have well matured crops, green fields and abundance of good water, while neighboring towns suffer for the want of them.

NOTE E—PAGE 31.   THE ACT OF OUTLAWRY.

This was intitled, "An Act to prevent the return to this State of certain persons therein named, and others who have left this State, or either of the United States, and joined the enemies thereof."

The Preamble recites a long list of names beginning with Thomas Hutchinson Esq. late Gov. of this state, and Francis Bernard lately Governor, and included Isaac Royal of Medford and John Chandler of Worcester, describes their offence and expresses the apprehension that many dangers may accrue to this State and the United States, should they be again admitted to reside here; it is therefore enacted that should either of them return, he shall be "transported to some port or place within the dominions, or in the possession of the forces of the king of Great Britain, as soon as may be;" and, returning again without liberty from the General Court, shall, on conviction, "suffer the pains of death, without benefit of clergy."

NOTES D AND F—PAGES 30 AND 33.   PROPRIETOR'S RECORDS.

A duplicate copy of these "entered from the original and compared therewith," by the Proprietor's Clerk, together with a copy of the plan of their lands, taken after the final division into lots, are in our archives. The largest of the aforesaid copies brings down the doings of the Proprietors to their last meeting in 1787; whereas the other closes May 30, 1774; our references are to the first named copy.

These documents are worthy of careful preservation. as illustrating our early history, and the character of the men who undertook the settlement of this then waste corner of Worcester County. Through a long series of meetings, extending over many years, and bridging two periods of protracted war, these men were prompt in their attendance upon the business, and earnest and liberal in their policy of bringing forward this settlement. From the day they paid down their first installment. until their corporate existence ceased, there were plenty of assessments on their shares for the payment of expenditures, while their dividends were not only few and far between, but also very small.

The records designate two divisions of these lands. The first consisted of seventeen 200 acre lots appropriated for the settlement of the 60 families and the public lots required by the conditions of the sale and called the "settler's division" or "first division." These lots were located in different parts of the purchase in such manner as the committee judged would best subserve the interests alike of proprietors and settlers. The public square of ten acres is also to be added, and we have the amount of land, in addition to their purchase money, and all their time, labor and assessments, appropriated to fulfill the conditions of the sale.

In the "second division," (called also "the Proprietors part" or "division,") the residue of the land was also laid out in 200-acre lots, where it could be done, and in other cases the contents of the smaller lots were expressed. The meadow lands, however, were laid out in 10 acre lots, so far as the committee judged them worth the expense of surveying; and a special committee was chosen to "qualify" the lots, by so "coupling a good lot and a poorer lot together that justice be done to each proprietor in the drawing of the lots." "A fair plan of this division was to be made out, and "returned to the Proprietors in order to be recorded."

When all this was so done, the Proprietors, at a meeting June 7, 1765, and before proceeding to draw for lots, appropriated to the first settled minister, for the ministry, and the school, in addition to the 100 acres already set apart for each, the following lots,—to the minister "the lot No. 63, containing 166 acres, and the lot No. 75, containing 165 acres."—for the ministry, "the lot No. 68, containing 200 acres, and the lot No. 114, containing 144 acres, and the lot No. 32, containing 80 acres,"— for the school, the lot No. 2, containing 193 acres, the lot No. 89, containing 85 acres, and the lot No. 30, containing 142 acres. All these lots were in the second, or Proprietors' division.

And here we have the origin of the old ministerial, and school funds, these lands having been, at length, sold by the town, and their proceeds invested, and the yearly income of which still perpetuates the influence of these Proprietors, in these directions

Most of the other lots in this division, and one lot (No, 8) in the settlers' part, in exchange for which, two lots of 100 acres each, had been laid out the year before, were drawn by the several Proprietors, and became their individual property. The residue remained as common and undivided lands; and in 1770 these meetings began to be called, not in the name of " the Proprietors of Royalston," but " the Proprietors of the common and undivided lands lying in Royalston.

NOTE G.—PAGE 33.   OUR CHARTER.

†*Anno Regni Regis Georgii Tertii Quinto.*†—An act for erecting a town in the county of Worcester by the name of Royalston:

Whereas the Proprietors of the land lying north of Athol, within the county of Worcester, known by the name of Royalston, have petitioned this Court, that, for the reasons mentioned, said land may be incorporated into a Town, and vested with the powers and authority belonging to the other Towns, for the encouragement of said settlement.—

Be it enacted by the Governor, Council, and House of Representatives that said tract of land bounded and described as follows viz: Beginning at a pillar of stones on the province line, the northwest corner, and from thence running south by the east line of Warwick five miles and two hundred and ninety three rods to a pillar of stones, the southwest corner, and from thence running east with the north line of Athol five miles and two hundred and sixty five rods to a red oak and a heap of stones, the northeast corner of Athol and from thence south by the east line, of Athol one mile and one hundred and ninety rods to a stake and stones, a corner of Templeton, and from thence east three degrees south one mile and eighty six rods by said Templeton, to the southwest corner, and from thence north twelve degrees east five miles and eighty rods on the west line of Winchendon to a heap of stones, the northwest corner of said Winchendon, and thence east twelve degrees south six miles and sixty rods by the north line of said Winchendon to the northeast corner thereof, and from thence north twelve degrees east by the west line of Dorchester Canada two hundred and ninety five rods to the province north bounds, and from thence by the province line fourteen miles and two hundred and eighty five rods to the corner first mentioned, Be and hereby is enacted into a Town, by the name of Royalston, and the inhabitants thereof shall have and enjoy all such immunities and privileges as other Towns in this province have and do by law enjoy. And be it further enacted that Joshua Willard Esq., be and hereby is empowered to issue his warrant to some principal inhabitant, of said Town of Royaston requiring him, in his Majesty's name, to warn and notify the said inhabitants qualified to vote in Town affairs to meet together at such time and place, in said Town, as shall be appointed in said warrant, to choose such officers as the law directs, and may be necessary to manage the affairs of said Town, and the inhabitants so met shall be and are hereby empowered to choose officers accordingly.—And be it further enacted that all those persons that have already agreed to settle in said Township, and have given their bonds to perform the same, shall be accounted as part and parcel of said inhabitants, and be allowed to vote in their Town Meetings, in all Town affairs, as fully as those who actually live upon their settlement in said Town, and shall be accordingly taxed for the purposes aforesaid.

In Council Jan. 31, 1765, read a first time. In Council February 1, 1765, read a second time, and passed to be engrossed. Sent down for concurrence. Jno. Cotton, D. Secretary. In the House of Representatives February 14, 1765. Read three several times and concurred

S. WHITE, Speaker.

Saturday, February 16, 1765. An engrossed bill, entitled an act for erecting a Town in the county of Worcester, by the name of Royalston, having passed the House of Representatives to be enacted.

In Council read a third time, and passed in concurrence to be enacted.

Commonwealth of Massachusetts, Secretary's Department, Boston, July 1, 1865.

A true copy from the Archives and Records.
OLIVER WARNER,
SECRETARY OF THE COMMONWEALTH.

NOTE II.—PAGE 34.   EARLY SETTLERS.

Even the names of some of these have doubtless fallen out, alike from record and memory; while not a few of those that remain admit of only imperfect, and often very uncertain illustration. We give such as we have been able to glean, and verify in some good degree. Convenience in locating the settlers, rather than the order of their coming in, has determined the arrangement of this note, which, like the settlement of the town itself, covers quite a number of years.

Rev. Joseph Lee, has appropriate notice on pages 37-39. The old parsonage still stands at the head of the common, though with an addition on the east side. Thomas J. Lee. Esq. succeeded his father on the estate, and is referred to pages 59-60. The house and lands, since his removal, have had various proprietors. None of the family remain in town. A son, Capt. Sam'l Lee, of Templeton, was one of our Vice Presidents on centennial day.

Capt. Peter Woodbury settled next south, on the Athol road; had a large family of sons and daughters, 10 of whom lived to have families of their own; kept a public house many years; d. 1806, æ. 70; was succeeded by his S. Capt. Daniel, who m. Esther, D. of Jonathan Waite; he was succeeded by his S. Peter, who still lives upon the place, having settled his sons,

George, and James P. on this early and still excellent farm, now furnished with two dwelling houses, and good out-buildings.

Capt. Woodbury is represented among us, not only by grand children and great grand children, but by descendants in families not bearing his name. It is related of him, that, probably on the occasion of the Burgoyne alarm, he marched into the meeting house in time of divine service, and gave out this military order, "Every man belonging to my company, turn out."

There were several large and early families west of this place, in a section now given up to wood and pasture land. *Jona. Waite* lived just upon the height of land back of Woodbury's. Here Capt. Daniel found his wife, as did some other young men. The family at length removed from town; and the place was, for a time, occupied by various persons. *Thomas Beale* was one of them—a name once familiar in town. *Obadiah Walker*, from Douglas, brought up a large family on a place further west; m. Nancy McCullock of Barre, was one of the *first* settlers. His sons, Obadiah and Elijah, settled in town, and descendants of both still remain with us. His D., Martha, m. Ephraim Hill. He d. in Croydon, N. H. 1810, æ. 90. *Cornelius Putnam*, from Sutton, was a neighbor of Walker; had a large family, but removed from town, and *David Sweet*, became proprietor of a part, or all, of these two farms; and though he left none to represent him in town, we still have his name in the Sweet lot in this vicinity.

South of Capt. Woodbury's on the Athol road, we next find the settlement of *Ezekiel Cutler*, supposed to have come from Sutton. He is said to have inaugurated cider-making in Royalston; d. 1800 æ. 64; was succeeded by his S. Ezekiel, whose children were all, or mostly, born here. The family removed from town, and the place, after passing through several hands, is now owned by N. Wilson Bragg.

Dea. Benj. Woodbury settled the next place, south. He organized with the 1st Cong. Church here, Oct. 13, 1766; was one of its first deacons; d. 1793, æ. 68. Daniel Hubbard occupied this place for many years.

Benajah Woodbury, settled farther south, at the foot of the hill, where Artemas Raymond now lives; d. 1802, æ. 55. These three Woodburys were brothers, and from Sutton. Only the first named has now representatives in town.

The "settlers lot," No. 16, lay next south, and is inscribed, on the Proprietors' Plan, with the name of "Stockwell." We suppose that Abraham, Moses, and Daniel Stockwell, each had a family on this lot. One of their settlements was where Sullivan Raymond now lives. It is said that the others settled over the hill, west from this farm.

Benj. Marsh built a grist and saw mill on the site originally selected for this purpose, by the Proprietors, near the falls on the Lawrence. He received a title to the "mill lot," south, and adjoining the falls, with other encouragements, and gave his bond to build, and maintain, suitable mill accommodations; but failing to meet the conditions of his bond, the Proprietors recovered £200, in a suit at law; a part of which they afterwards remitted. He sold and moved from town.

Isaac Gale, from Sutton, succeeded him; but d. 1779, æ. 48. He was the ancestor of the Gales, who since have been numerous and highly respected in town. His S. Isaac, father of Isaac, Jonathan and Otis, settled in the east part of the town, and their families settled about him. His S. Jonathan, settled in the west part of the town, and was long a neighbor of his brother-in-law, Lt. Daniel Peck, who m. his sister, Dilly. These early mills were on the site now occupied by Sullivan Raymond, and Son's old saw mill, and pail shop. The *mill lot* has several proprietors at the present time.

Nathaniel Bragg, settled south of this lot, and adjoining Athol; m. a Miss Wilson from Barre; was of English descent, and ancestor of all of his name in town; d. 1818 æ. 72; was succeeded by his S. Nathaniel, whose widow still lives near the old house spot, with a daughter; and whose sons, N. Wilson, and Henry O. Bragg, are the proprietors of most of their father, and grand father's land. Benj. brother of Nathaniel Jr., built a carding mill, afterwards converted into a satinet factory, north of the falls, and lived and died in this neighborhood. His second wife survives him, and three of his children live in town.

In the early times, the road leading directly south from the common by the east side of the school house, was quite populous; but now is without inhabitants. We here indicate some of the settlements.

William Town located just north of the Lawrence meadows, on the east side of the road. He brought up a large family; was one of the *first* settlers; "embodied" with the Cong'l Church in 1766; was a prominent and respected citizen; d. 1811, æ. 80; was succeeded by his S. Moses, who sold to Isaac Whitmore. The place has since had several proprietors.

Samuel Putnam, from Sutton, and *David Copeland*, settled west of this road, and north of the Lawrence meadows. The latter had a Tannery, vestiges of which may still be seen. His name too, still adheres to the land he once owned; but none of these families, or their descendants are known to reside among us.

Lenox Tites, settled some distance south of the Lawrence, at the corner of the roads—Ashbel Goddard's old place; William, S. of Capt. Gad Pierce, subsequently owned the place; and after him, Ashbel Goddard, who m. Betsey, d. of William Pierce. He still owns the place, though now residing upon the common. On the west road from this corner was the settlement of *Nahum Green*, mentioned on pages 51, 52. A marble slab is in preparation to mark the solitary, and long neglected grave of this early patriot.

Capt. Jonathan Sibley, from Sutton, settled next west, and adjoining Green's. In 1763, he bought, and prepared his farm for settlement; the next year brought on his wife, two cows and a pair of steers. The wild beasts soon made way with one of his steers. He became a substantial farmer and valuable citizen; d. 1810, æ. 70; his wife died only a few weeks before; was succeeded by his S. Jonathan, after whose death the farm was sold to Jonathan Gale, who m. Patty Pierce. Since his death the place has been turned into pasturage, owned by his son, Dana, and son-in-law, Tarrant Cutler, and still called the Gale lot. The widow of Jonathan Sibley, Jr. built the house on the common, now owned by John Pierce, where she resided till her death, in 1853 æ. 92. The *Ellis* place, near Athol line, on the south road from Ashbel Goddard's farm, was early settled and till recently has been occupied by descendants of the original proprietor, Ezekiel Ellis.

Returning from this depopulated region, and passing down the common on the west side, we have next south of the present meeting-house, the settlement of the *Drs. Bacheller*, father and son, specially noticed page 46. This ancient residence, modernized and beautified, is now, with the land attached, owned and occupied, by Chauncy Chase, S. of David Chase, the oldest S. of Lt. Francis Chase, who m. Caroline, D. of Russel Morse, Sen.

Ebenezer Elliot, settled north of the original common. His house stood hard by the old town pump; D. 1794. This place, together with other lands north, was bought by Capt. William Raymond, from Athol, who built the house now owned and occupied by Ashbel Goddard, and gave the town the land by which the common was extended to his residence. He was the immediate ancestor of the Raymond's at the south part of the town. His father, Edward Raymond, lived and died with him. Edward was S. of Solomon Raymond, who came from England, settled in Bedford, and was a Revolutionary soldier. A cancelled Treasury note of $450, received by the said Solomon for his services, is now in the hands of our townsman, Joseph Raymond, Esq., a *souvenir* of his great grand father.

Joel and *Benj. Winship*, settled on the road leading from the northwest corner of the common. Their buildings stood about midway on the east side of the late Stephen P. White's pasture. They were the first men that died in town; and both by violent deaths. Joel perished in the cold, Jan. 21st, 1765. He was found dead, in the road east of Capt. Woodbury's, near where the tomb now stands, with part of a deer he had killed in the S. W. part of the town. The next year his brother Benj. was killed near his house, by the falling of a tree.

Jonah Hill, from Douglas, one of the first settlers, located north; house stood near the S. E., corner of Joseph Estabrook's pasture, m., Esther Livermore; his daughter, Abigail, is claimed as the *first-born* of Royalston. His S., Oliver, settled on the home farm: Mr. Hill settled his S., Ephraim, and his son-in-law. Elijah Walker, on a 200 acre lot, in the west part of the town, bought of the Proprietors. Ephraim Hill m., Martha, sister of Elijah Walker, who married the aforesaid Abigail Hill. Jonah Hill d., 1806, æ. 69.

Jason Babcock, settled west of Hill's; his house stood near the S. E., corner of George Woodbury's pasture; was taken captive by the Indians, while living in Athol, and carried to Canada. After getting safely back he removed to Royalston with his family. Katurah, a daughter, æ. 15, was killed by lightning, Aug. 30, 1769. She was watching from a window, the return of the people from church, it being the Sabbath. The only other cases in town, of death by lightning, of which we learn, occurred in 1845, and in the house on the adjoining Hill farm. The victims were two young persons, John H. C. Nichols, and a daughter of James Pierce. They were instantly killed by the same bolt. The last three settlements now deserted.

Benj. Hutchinson, from Sutton, settled next north of the Hill place, was succeeded by his S., Joshua, whose heirs lately sold the place to Joseph Raymond Esq. who, after putting the buildings in excellent repair, has settled his S., A. Dwight Raymond.

upon the farm. The elder Hutchinson was a carpenter; buildings put up by him between 90 and 100 yrs. ago are still standing. In repairing his farm house Mr. Raymond left one of the chambers as originally *finished*,—a specimen of the taste, patience, and workmanship, of this ancient *joiner*.

Ephraim Whitney, known also as Elder Whitney, settled north of this place on the old road now discontinued, as is also the settlement itself. This place had been previously opened and occupied by Daniel Pike. Lucy Whitney, D. of the elder, m., Abijah Richardson Jr. who succeeded his father Abijah on his place, Ephraim W. S., of Abijah and Lucy Richardson, after graduating with much promise, died just as he was entering upon the ministry. Another S., Andrew J. was a captain in the late war, and still another, Jefferson, died on his voyage home from the war.

Timothy Richardson, from Wrentham, settled next north, built near where Benj. W. Upham now lives. His first wife, Alice Wyman, was a relative of the gallant Seth Wyman, who, after the fall of Capt. Lovewell and his Lieut. commanded in the bloody "Lovewell fight;" and, by some historians, is made the hero of that celebrated personal encounter with the Indian-chief, Paugus. Mr. Richardson and his wife were original members of the 1st Congregational Church in Royalston. He was Royalston's first Representative in the General Court; settled several of his sons around him, and this whole section used to throng with his descendants. Abijah settled on the home-lot, and lived where Benj. W. Upham now lives. Eliphalet settled where Joseph R. Eaton now lives. Timothy, Jr. settled where his S., the late Stephen Richardson, lived. There Timothy Sen. d. 1801, æ. 87; here his S., Timothy d., and here also, Stephen, the S., of Timothy Jr. d., 1863, æ. 84.

Samuel Felch Jr. from Reading, settled the place, perhaps already opened, where now Russel Morse Jr. lives. His father, Samuel, and his brothers, Caleb and Nathan, seem to have removed to town about the same time; and all of them appear to have had settlements and families in this part of the town. The father is supposed to have lived near the pail shop of Horace Pierce and Son. His wife, Eunice, d., 1792, æ. 69. In 1795, he, being 76, m., Elizabeth Walton, æ. 70. He d., 1803, æ. 82. Caleb Felch m., Mary Chase, D.. of Lieut. Francis Chase 1788, She d., 1798, æ., 35. He settled on the place now owned by Wm. Fordice Bigelow, his dwelling house standing some 60 rods north of the present buildings. Nathan Felch had a family in town, but we cannot locate him. Lieut., Samuel Felch, S., of Samuel Felch Jr. carried on the mill on the Moore place, so called, within the recollection of some of our citizens. Some of this name removed to Fitzwilliam. William, a S., of Caleb, removed to Reading, Vermont, where a flourishing village bears the name of Felchville, from him. We have none of this name now in town, and whether 'they've remov'd or died,' we are in the same doubt as the Bi-centennial Poet of Reading, Mass., from. whence they came, who thus poetizes:

"Of Reuben Eaton, I must quote
One entertaining anecdote;
He lived within those cottage walls,
Where Adam Hawkes the senior dwells;
A place that once was occupied
By *Felches, who're remov'd or died.*"

Thomas Perry,—father of Micah, Thaddeus and Asa, all of whom had families in town, but as difficult of location as were the Felches,—settled the place now owned by Russel Morse, Sen. He sold to Dea. Ammi Falkner, who was to support him. He became quite infirm, and at times somewhat deranged. On the night of Jan. 10, 1810, he left his room, and wandered about in the snow and cold until he died, æ. 91. Dea. Falkner m., Anna, D. of Wm. Town. She d., 1817, æ. 57, and the Dea. m., for his second wife, the widow of Jonas Brewer, Sen. He ultimately removed to Milbury, where he lived and died with his son, Cyrus. The present proprietor, Mr. Morse, with the companion of his youth, is spending the evening of his long and industrious life in competency, surrounded with children and children's children.

Maj. John Norton, from Reading, settled the next place north. m., Margaret, D., of Dea. John Bacheller. He sold to Capt. Isaac Metcalf. The place has since had different proprietors, and is now owned by Albion Mosman.   Maj. Norton, after several removals, finally bought and built upon the place now owned by Wm. W. Clement, where he died.   He was in the Revolutionary War, and fought in the trenches with Lieut. Jonas Work and Wm. Clement, soldiers from this town, in the battle of Bunker Hill. His S., Thomas, of Portland Me., was one of our Vice Presidents at the Centennial.

John Bacheller, Maj., Esq. and Dea., from Reading, settled north and adjoining the place last mentioned. His house stood on the opposite side and a little South of the residence of Sam'l. Morse, the present proprietor: He was born in Haverhill. m., Margaret Swain of Reading, 1766. He removed to Royalston from Reading, bringing his wife and five children, six more were subsequently added to this number. He buried his wife in 1810 and removed to Warwick, to live with his S., Thomas, where he died. Hannah, the first of his family born in town, m., Jonas Bartlett, and is now the sole survivor of her father's, and her own family [10 children] with the exception of her son, John N. Bartlet, with whom she now lives, enjoying the use of her physical and mental powers in a remarkable degree, though in her 89th year. Her Mother was an immediate descendent of the Appleton family, of Ipswich, among whom are found the "Bleeders," so called. Mr. Bartlett, has furnished us with a note, illustrating this phenomenon; which will be found under its appropriate title, "Bleeders."

Elisha Cheney, settled next north, [the place may have been opened before] where he kept tavern and store for sometime.

This place has been in many hands since; the last two having been Noah Miles, who died on the place, and his S., Henry, the present proprietor who succeeded him.

Silas Heywood, settled on the west road from this corner. His farm adjoined the State Line. His family was one of the sufferers in the epidemic of 1795,—refered to page 60—five of the children dying that year. He was succeeded by his S., Silas, who sold to his brother Benj., who exchanged with Moses Nichols for the Felch farm, on which he erected the present buildings. He afterwards sold and removed to Fitzwilliam, where he lately died. *Moses Nichols,* S., of Henry or *"Landlord* Nichols," m. Sally Beals, for his first wife, Sarah Whitney of Littleton, for his second, and Mehitable Cutler for his third. His S., Henry, now occupies the place.

There were several other early settlements east from these last places. *Ebenezer Goodell's* adjoined the Felch, or Bigelow farm. *Jonas Lewis* lived east of the Lawrence, and probably built the first saw-mill on the site of Horace Pierce & Son's pail shop. Other names are given, and vestiges pointed out in this region, but we are unable to illustrate them. Here, too, east of the pail shop, we have *Tory hill,* with its various and conflicting traditions, the most probable of which, perhaps, is, that certain Tories, fleeing before popular indignation, made an old building on the unfrequented bridle-road over the hill, their refuge for a time. It is said they were driven off by the strategy of one man, who, for the sport of the thing, came upon the house in the night, armed with a musket, and bidding his men stand firm and take the Tories, dead or alive, called upon them to surrender. There was a rush from the side and rear windows, and the flight of the fugitives was hastened by the discharge of the musket; and that was the last of these interlopers in Royalston, —all which is clearly possible, while it appears a very proper reason for the name of this hill, which were otherwise hard to be accounted for.

Joseph Emerson, from Reading, settled where A. F. Tenny now lives; was a Revolutionary pensioner; m. Rebecca Nichols; he and his wife d. 1837, æ. respectively 86, and 87; was succeeded by his S., Dea. Joseph Emerson; who sold to Dea. Lot Richardson, who m. Polly, D., of the original settler. The present proprietor m. Mary, D., of Dea. Richardson. Elias, another son of the original settler, lived where his S., Wm. H. Emerson now lives.

Joseph Eves, said to have been a deserter from Burgoyne's army, settled east of Emerson; died 1797, æ. 46, leaving a widow and an adopted son, Joseph, on the place. The widow m. Solomon Eager, from Warwick, and died here at an advanced age. The adopted son married Dinah Eager; whose son, Joseph, now resides in Dublin, New Hampshire. A daughter m. Simeon Bosworth of this town. This is now known as the Eager place, but deserted.

Benj. Leathe, from Reading, settled next south from Emerson. m. Lois Walton, of Reading; is said to have participated in that original and historic "Tea Party" in Boston harbor, and to have served in the Revolution; was succeeded by his son, Benj., who lately died upon the place. The farm now owned by Amos M. Lamb,—John, a son of Benj. Leathe, Sen. owns the Nathan Cutting place.

John Fry, Capt. Esq. and Dea., illustrated on page 35, was an original member of the Cong'l Church and one of its first deacons. His grandsons, John and the late Benj. Fry, occupied the two present substantial farm-houses upon this place, still the property of the immediate descendants of the original settler.

The south and east slopes of this hill, beautiful for situation and of excellent soil, have afforded homesteads for numerous families, first and last; but the changes are not now within our power of illustration. *John Holman*, S., of Edward, though not the first settler, once owned the farm, now the property of Barnet Bullock, Esq, and transmitted it to his S., Dea. Seth Holman.

lately deceased. The latter afterwards lived where Dea. Maynard Partridge now lives, and carried on the mills there. His widow and S., Seth N. Holman, now live at the corner of the roads, south of the Fry place. *Silvanus Heminway*, from Sudbury, probably, settled east of the Bullock place, on the old road, and where Dr. Richardson afterwards lived for a time. He owned a large tract of land, extending south nearly to the Winchendon road. He was a prominent citizen; had a large family; was delegate, in 1779, to the Convention, which framed the Constitution of Massachusetts. Neither his family, nor name, so far as we can learn, is now represented in town.

Nathan Brigham Newton first settled on the west bank of the Lawrence, near where Dea. Patridge now lives. He afterwards removed and located on the high lands east of the river where now stands the goodly farm house and buildings of his son Col. Elmer Newton. He married Mary Stewart; had a family of twelve children, and became one of our largest land holders; d. 1843, æ. 84; his wife, d. 1842, æ. 82. Col. now Dea. Elmer Newton, the only survivor of this large family, with the exception of a widowed sister, is the present proprietor of this fine estate. This early family remains honorably represented and connected in our present population.

William Brown, from Reading, first settled the Prouty place, and established a tannery there, then bought of Elder Whitman Jacobs the place south and adjoining Newton's, where, as is supposed, Abel Whitney first settled. In several purchases he annexed to his farm the Thomas Heminway place farther south, and became a large landed proprietor. In his advancing years, like his neighbor Newton, he settled his son, Col. Benj. Brown with him and died here 1830, æ. 72; his wife d. 1851, æ. 90. Col. Brown commanded the Royalston grenadiers, when they marched for the defence of Boston in the last war with England. He, too, has lately settled his son Lt.

Benj. H. Brown, with him on this well conditioned farm; remitting, at his discretion, care and labor to younger heads and hands.

Thomas Heminway, whose place south of this has now become a part of the Brown farm as above stated, was an early settler with a family of sons and daughters, all of whom are gone.

Jon'n. Cutler, from Sutton, settled on the west corner of the roads north of Newton's, but, later in life, he bought the Daniel Moody place, and settled there with his S., Tarrant, where he d. 1826, æ. 90. Tarrant m. Lydia Whitney. He was succeeded by his S. Tarrant, the present proprietor, several of whose brothers settled abroad, and among them, Lysander, now residing in Milwaukee, Wis., who entered the late war as Col., rose to Brig. Gen. and now, for meritorious service, ranks as Maj. Gen. by brevet.

Lt. James Work settled on the east corner of the roads and opposite to Cutler's first settlement. He was a companion in arms with Major Norton and William Clement at the battle of Bunker hill. His D. Sally, married William Pierce, S. of Capt. Gad Pierce, and his D. Betsey, married William Chase, son of Lt. Frances Chase, and he is at present represented in town by the descendants of these families; d. 1783, æ. 40. His widow m. Alexander Parkman Davis of Templeton, by whom she had other children. She and her second husband died upon this place. These adjoining farms are now discontinued.

Bezaleal Barton settled next north of these farms, built a grist mill on the Lawrence west of his house, where now stands the Moore saw mill, so called; d. in Camp at Charlestown, 1775, æ. 50. This place has passed through several hands since; the mill and lands adjoining, have been detatched from the original farm which is now the property of the heirs of the late Col. Willard Newton, and occupied by his son, Horatio D. Newton.

Samuel Barton, who with his wife Hannah organized with the Cong'l Church in 1766, and was a Revolutionary Soldier, and

Benj. Barton, who married Mehitable Fry, in 1769, we are unable to locate.

John Black settled on the Winchendon road east from the Cutler and Work corners, near where school house No. 2, now stands.

. *Lt. Francis Chase,* from Sutton, settled on this road, at the next corner north, on the site of the Doane place, so called. m. Mary Perkins of Sutton, died on his way from Boston, probably in a fit, 1791, æ. 55. He and one or more of his sons, were called out during the war, probably on the occasion of the Burgoyne invasion. David, his eldest son, after living awhile in district No. 8, a place now discontinued, succeeded his father. His wife was Sarah Raymond of Athol. He d. 1816, æ. 55. His son Chauncy now lives on the common. William Chase, brother of David, who married Betsey Work, settled on the place now owned by his son, George Chase, and is represented in town by Capt. William, Francis Chase, and other families. Elizabeth, daughter of Lt. Chase, was lost in the woods, when three or four years old, and not recovered till after a search of several days. Mrs. Black, a neighbor, found her in the cornfield eating green corn. When returned to the family the father, for the first time, during all those terrible days, gave way to tears. The child related that she had "eaten some berries, seen the bear trap and men with dogs and guns. but they was n't her father, and she hid;" she afterwards m. Eliphalet Richardson, and died at the age of 86. Her daughter Mrs. Betsey Eaton, the venerable mother of a member of this committee, lives with her son, Joseph R. Eaton, on her father's place. Mr. Eaton well remembers that, when a boy, aged men used to call upon his grandmother and talk over the incidents of that exciting hunt. in which they were participators.

Jonas Thompson, from Holden, settled next north; m. Margaret Beath of Worcester; d. 1816, æ. 72. Capt. Robert Thompson, his son, succeeded him; d. 1864, æ. 91, having previously settled his son, Orrin, the present proprietor, upon the place. This is one of our large and valuable farms, always having been conducted by intelligent and practical farmers and highly respectable citizens.

Lt. Oliver Work, supposed to be brother of Lt. James Work, settled next east of Lt. Francis Chase, on the Winchendon road. He m. for his first wife Sarah Heminway, in 1780. She d. 1788, æ. 32; and he m. Hannah Cutler in 1789. He d. 1793, æ. 48. This place was afterwards owned and occupied by Sam'l Gregory. Then by Capt. Wm. Chase. Since he left it, it has had several proprietors, and now, lately, has shared the fate of Poland, being partitioned and incorporated with the farms adjacent. Only the barn and cellar-hole remain to tell of this once flourishing settlement.

David and Joel Taft, John Wood and Levi Fiske, all from Upton, bought 329 acres, at $2,00 per acre, lying east from the last named place,—constituting a part of the "Pierpont Grant." This purchase was divided into four lots, upon which, however, they continued to work in company, till they had each (save Fiske, who sold out to Wood) prepared homes for their prospective families. Two of them found wives among the daughters of the land, whither they had come to dwell. David Taft, m. Eunice, D., of Lt. Jonas Allen; and Wood m. Zerriah, D., of Capt. Peter Woodbury. Joel Taft, also, soon became a housekeeper. Such was the origin of the Taft and Wood farms; each of which have added wealth and population to the town. The Taft farms are now dismantled of dwellings, and either absorbed in other farms, or occupied by non-residents as pasture lands &c. But the Wood farm continues to flourish; and the present proprietor, lately come into possession, gives promise of sustaining its reputation. He is the eldest S. of John Wood, Esq. who d. 1863, æ. 50; and who was one of our best, and most enterprising farmers, and a useful, as now a lamented citizen. He succeeded his father, the original settler. His excellent widow lives with her S. Henry S. When this farm was first taken up there was serious apprehension lest it might prove deficient in enduring water, and in the *quantity* of stones. This doubt, long since dispelled, can scarcely fail to excite a smile, especially in regard to the last particular, while surveying the massive walls that enclose the well sustained fields, and the large crop of well grown stones, turned out by crow bars and oxen at every successive " breaking up."

Silas Bowker settled east of these farms, and near the Priest brook, probably on part of the " Priest Grant." His S. Stephen, settled the Bowker place, so called; and the father ultimately removed, and closed his life with his S. Stephen, was succeeded by his S. Nathaniel, whose widow, and S., Ch. W. Bowker, now occupy this excellent farm, continued under good cultivation, and furnished with substantial and commodious buildings.

Joseph Priest, illustrated p. 27, took the precaution of making a sort of castle, or, to express ourselves less romantically, *blockhouse* of his residence. We suspect that his small defensive provisions, constituted all the material there is for the tradition of a *fort* in this region. Another tradition has some currency, and perhaps more solid ground to stand upon. It is said that one of the committees for viewing this new territory, and preparing the way for settlement, brought on a small package of choice tea, and, putting up at this house, left it with the hostess in the morning with the request, that she would prepare some for their refreshment, at the evening meal, when they returned from their tramp. The good woman did so, cooking the whole of the fragrant parcel, as a seasoning, along with the " boiled-dish." But if this ancient dame did not understand the most approved mode of tea-making, a descendant of hers, Miss N. A. W. Priest, born in town, but now a resident in Winchendon, can make good poetry; as her beautiful Hymn, " Over the River," demonstrates. It is worthy of the place it now holds among the "Hymns of the Ages," published by Ticknor & Co. Boston, Second Series.

In the neighborhood of this proto-settler of our territory, there have been several large families, and good farms, though most of them were more modern, than fall within the design of these illustrations. Since the advent of Rail-roads, however, the travel has been taken off from the turn-pike, passing through this section, seriously affecting the thrift of this part of the town.

About a mile south of Priest's we come to another early settler, *Jon'a. Bosworth, Jr.* He located on the west bank of Priest's brook just south of the Winchendon road, and where Ch. M. Flagg now lives; m. Mary Holt, said to have been the first person born within the limits of Winchendon. They had 14 children, some of whom still live, and not a few of their posterity. This settler came from Lunenburg in company with his father, Jon'n. who settled in the west part of the town, where Marshall Herrick now lives. Jon'n. Jr. d., 1818. æ., 70; his wife, 1847, æ., 93. Bosworth is said to have had a lively time with the wolves, one night; being set upon by a pack of them, as he was returning home through the woods. He had with him a lighted torch, and, as they pressed upon him, he would turn and rush among them with his flaming pine knot, scattering them in wild affright. He continued this manœuver till he reached a place of safety. According to one version, he took refuge upon a huge boulder, that lies to this day hard by the south side of the road, nearly in the line of Col. Arnold's late residence, from the top of which he hurled defiance upon his baffled, and howling foes, till day-light admonished them to disperse.

Nathan Cutting settled about two miles west of Bosworth; was one of the *first* settlers; spent the winter of 1762—63, quite alone, in a house, or *place*, sunk partly into the hill, east of John Leathe's, looking out upon the meadows. A thrifty young apple-tree now grows in the heart of this excavation. It should be grafted with some choice fruit, and made to *bear* up this early name. Cutting got this dwelling so comfortable that he occupied it for some years after he was married; but ultimately built upon the site of John Leathe's house, the present proprietor. His barn, upon the opposite side of the road, put up by Benj. Hutchinson, still stands, only having been in part new-silled, boarded below, and shingled, and bids fair to outlast many more modern, but less substantial structures. This settler d. 1821, æ. 80. Mrs. Hiram Harrington, a grand daughter, and her children, are his only descendants, in town, as we suppose.

Lieut. Jonas Allen, formerly written *Alliene,* settled west of this place, at the corner of the roads beyond the Bowker farm. His father came to town with him, and d., 1786, æ., 86. The Lieut., built a saw-mill north of his house, where now Lyman Stone's mill stands; was a prominent man, and at the head of an interesting family. He was a very early settler; d. 1822, æ., 93. Lucy, a D. of his, d. 1858, æ., 84, the last of the family in town. The mill and lands adjoining, were long since detached from this farm, which has had many owners since it passed out of the hands of the Allens. Liberty Holt is its present proprietor.

Silas Cutting, settled next north of the mill, above named. He d. while abroad in the war, 1777. Like Allen, and Nathan Cutting, he "embodied" with the 1st. Cong'l. Ch. in 1766. He is supposed to have lived on, or near the site of the house now occupied by Edwin Hadley, formerly occupied for some time by Joshua Cummings, father of Lt. Col. Charles Cummings, and of Rev. Henry Cummings, whose names appear in subsequent notes.

Amos Jones, settled next north; came in during 1763; and of whom a Moose story is told. He was out looking up his cattle, and hearing a crashing among the under brush, supposed them to be at hand; but instead of his cattle a huge Moose came forth and confronted him. His trusty gun soon made an end of the Moose, whose hide he afterwards converted into a pair of leather breeches, and a side-saddle. The breeches he wore himself; but upon the side-saddle he pursuaded one Lydia Woolly, to ride home with him, and take permanent possession of the saddle, and his domestic affairs. They had a fine family of children; and ultimately sold this place, and settled south of the Cutler farm, where their S. Silas Jones, now lives. He d. 1826. æ. 84. Silas, born 1780, became sole proprietor of this excellent farm, of which he gives the following among other items. He has raised 90 bushels of corn to the acre; two years in succession, harvested 400 bushels of corn, besides other grain; one year, having cleared a large wood lot, and put it into rye, he had 1200 bushels of rye, in addition to 400 bushels of other grain; once he slaughtered a cow from his own stall, whose net weight was 1025 lbs. The large and substantial farm house, barn, and other buildings to match, together with the fine stock of cattle, found on these premises, give countenance to these figures; but the rock-studded fields, might tempt one to question their accuracy. It was so with one of us; but the old farmer thought our scepticism worthy only of the, perhaps, personal remark, "Folks don't love to work as well as they used to, I think." The active farmer here now, is the S., Dea. Aaron Jones, though the father is still as busy as the day is long, especially in his fine garden, and among his large and profitable collection of grape vines, which cover not only arbor and trellis, but the massive walls about the farm, and in their season, glow with the bloom of the ripening clusters.

The original settlement of Amos Jones has now, for a generation, been the property of James Wilson, whose children have all settled abroad, and who now resides in Winchendon.

James Hubbard, from Rutland, bought the farm next north, previously commenced by Jon'n Pierce. The buildings stand at the corner of the road, north of the last named place. He was succeeded by his S., James, the present proprietor, whose children, as they settled in life, have removed from town.

John Osborne, about 1770, bought the Pro'ps. lot, No. 76, containing 133 acres, lying east of Hubbard's, and bounded on the east by the Pierpont Grant. The land cost him 9s. 6d. per acre. He d. 1792, æ. 49; and his place after several transfers, was bought in 1812, of Abel Downe by Amos Whitney, from Leominster, but whose father lived and died in Rindge, N. H. Mr. Whitney, m. Sophia Harris, of Fitchburg, and moved on to this place about 53 years ago. He has now settled his S., Levi, with him. His eldest S. Hon. George Whitney, the proprietor of the woolen factory, chair shop and other mills in So. Royalston, is now our heaviest business man and largest tax payer. He resides on the common.

Nathan Reed, from Rutland, settled on the north road from the corner east of Whitney's, where his family grew up. Later in life he sold this place, and bought a farm farther east, now the Whitmore place. His D., Betsey, m. Col. Benj. Brown. His S. Moses, lives in Winchendon. Another S. Capt. Cyrus B. Reed, is one of our good farmers and worthy citizens. John Holman, S. of Lt. Edward, and father of Dea. Seth Holman bought this place of Nathan Reed; and settled his S. John upon it; who d. here 1859, æ. 68. His heirs lately sold the place to Marcus Hobbs, the present occupant.

Jacob Hale, if not the first, was an early settler on the farm at the end of the south road, from the corner last named. It is now the valuable and well conducted farm of Solyman Heywood who m. Harriet, D., of Stephen, one of the youngest children of Lt. Edward Holman.

Joel Howard, the proprietor of the farm west of Heywood's, m. Comfort, D., of Jacob Hale.

William Clement, settled on the road leading to the common from Lt. Jonas Allen's place. The site of his house is a little west of the foot of the hill, and north of the road. He m. Anna, D., of Henry Nichols. Their children Isaac, Elizabeth, Sally, William, Mary, Dilly and Charlotte, were born here, and several of them settled in town,—Isaac m. Mary, D. of Wm. Town; Sally m. Isaac Prouty, who bought the farm and tannery, then lately established by Wm. Brown, and carried on both the tanning business and the farm; was succeeded by his S., Wm. H. Prouty, the present proprietor. The tannery was burnt some years ago, and has not been rebuilt; Elizabeth m. Asa, S., of Dr. Stephen Bacheller, Sen. and settled on the place next west of Prouty's—said to have been begun by Reuben Walker—The Dr. and his wife spent their last years here; and Asa Bacheller and his wife lately died upon the place, which is now owned by Franklin H. S. of Ashbel Goddard.

About 1810, Wm. Clement with a part of his family removed to Croydon, N. H. where he d. æ., 85. He was a soldier of the Revolution, and in the battle of Bunker Hill. His S., William, has returned to his native town, and is now living with his second wife, the widow of the second Dr. Bacheller, on the place next west of Franklin H. Goddard's. His S., Wm. W. Clement, our Representative elect to the next General Court, is the proprietor of the Maj. Norton place,—the last before reaching the common.

Lt. Nathan Wheeler settled next west of his compatriot, William Clement, Sen. He and his wife organized with the Cong'l. Ch. in 1766, They removed to Lincoln, N. H. about 1792; and the farm became the property of Capt. Gad Pierce. It is now better known as the Paul Pierce place; but, like the Clement place. it is without inhabitants, or habitations.

Capt. Gad Pierce, born in Harvard, 1741, m. Mary Foster of Acton, and removed to Royalston. He finally built on the west bank of the Lawrence, next east from Prouty's, where he opened a public house and had a good farm. He d. 1811, æ. 70, leaving his name upon this place to the present day. His name has heretofore been upholden by numerous and large families of his descendants; but at present only two distinct families of his name reside in town,—that of Horace Pierce, S. of Jonathan the "portly" post man, referred to on page, 62, and that of Capt.

George Pierce, S., of William. The daughters and granddaughters have dealt more kindly by the Captain; and we still number a goodly representation, who trace back their pedigree, to this settler, through their mothers,—as the Pipers, Gales, Turners, Goddards, Reeds and Bryants. Capt. William Pierce, from Acton, father of Capt. Gad, (whose given name was borne up by William, the father, and William, a brother of Capt. George Pierce,) and two other sons, Zebulun and Eliphalet, come to town with or soon after, Capt. Gad Pierce, and made settlements in this same neighborhood. But they all early removed, and left no representatives. The locality of Capt. William is still pointed out. It was on the west bank of the Lawrence, nearly east of the residence of his great-grandson, Capt. George Pierce, and on his land.

Henry, Isaac and William Nichols, from Sutton, had early settlements in town. *Henry* better known as "Landlord Nichols," took up the now conspicuous and flourishing farm of C. H. Maxham, where he kept a public house. Having lost his wife in 1781, he m. the widow of Isaac Gale, and subsequently, settling his S., Henry, on the home place, removed to the "mill lot," and carried on the mills near the "falls." Here he settled his S., Elijah, who built the house north of the falls, now occupied by Nathan Smith, and afterwards built upon the common next north of the Lee farm, where he d. 1856; æ. 83; and was succeeded by his S., Lt. Joseph T. Nichols, who m. Martha G. D., of the widow Mary Turner. Henry Nichols, Sen., d. 1814. æ. 83; the ancestor of all the Nichols families now in town. His S. Henry, lately deceased, left the homestead to C. H. Maxham the present proprietor. Isaac. settled south of his brother Henry, on the place now owned by Francis Chase. His house stood a short distance from the present residence. He organized with the Cong. Ch. in 1766; was chosen Deacon in 1781; and removed to Croydon, N. H., about 1790. His S. Isaac is one of those who are claimed as the *first born* of Royalston. We cannot enter into this controversy for precedence: but the evidence is indubitable that the children of Royalston, in those days, did mightily increase. Rev. Ammi Nichols, S. of the Deacon, born here, 1781, and who has been in the ministry upwards of 60 years, was present and one of the Vice Presidents on Centennial Day.—The Dea. Nichols' place, after his removal from town was owned a few years by David, S. of "Landlord Nichols." He sold to Abraham Eddy, whose father, Benj., once lived on the place now owned by Wm. F. Bigelow, and who had several daughters that married in town,—Hannah m. Abijah Richardson, Sally m. Henry Nichols, Jr., Nancy m. Willard Upham, father of Benjamin W. Upham, and Susannah m. Daniel Hubbard. Abraham, the S. above named, m. Sarah D., of Lt. Francis Chase, built the house on the place he bought of David Nichols. was succeeded by his S., Gibbs W. who sold to Francis Chase, the present proprietor. William Nichols bought the place settled by Bezaleal Barton, and carried on both the farm, and the mill on the Lawrence, west of his home. He went by the name of "Miller Nichols." When customers needed him at the mill, they rang a bell, suspended upon the premises, the signal for "Miller Nichols" to leave his farm duties, and attend to the callers under the hill.

Isaac Gregory, Lt. Esq. and Dea., settled east and adjoining the Henry Nichols place. He came from Templeton. This respected and useful citizen d. 1808. æ. 49. His S. Maj. Gen. Franklin Gregory, is commemorated on pages 62, 63. John P. Gregory, of Cambridge, was one of the Secretaries, and Charles A. Gregory, Esq. of Chicago, Ill., made a stirring speech at the Centennial dinner table,—sons of Gen. Gregory.

Along the road running east of the Gregory place, were several other early families. One, by the name of Armstrong, gave name to the stream, which crosses this road, and running north and then west, empties into the Lawrence. Timothy Armstrong, a soldier of the Revolution, and John Armstrong, who was killed by the falling of a tree, Oct. 9, 1787, are supposed to have been of this family. Abraham and Cæsar Toney, colored men, owned a place east of Armstrong's, and each had a family. David and Simeon Stockwell, sons of Joseph, owned the next two farms; and both are still represented among us by descendants. This road, however, is now discontinued, and no dwellings are to be found on these old localities.

Silas Chase, S. of Rogers, settled the place next south of Francis Chase, receiving the north part of his father's farm. He was succeeded by his S., Joseph W. Chase, who has now settled his S., Joseph W. upon the farm. The house was lately rebuilt.

Henry Bond, Delegate to the first Provincial Congress, 1774, and to the Concord Convention, 1779, settled next south, on the old road, lately "turned." He removed with his family, to Grafton, Vt., about 1794, and was succeeded immediately, or soon after, by David Lyon, who d. 1808, æ. 70. Subsequently William Eddy, S., of Abraham, bought this place, and after the road was "turned," moved his house upon the new road farther south and built a new barn. He sold to Lyman W. Seaver. The house was burned in 1864, and has not been rebuilt.

Lt. Nathan Bartlett, from Brookfield, settled next south; was succeeded by his S., Jonas, who m. Hannah, D., of Dea. John Bacheller. He was succeeded by his S., John N. Bartlett, the present proprietor. Nathan was a descendant of Henry, from Wales, who come to this country about 1700, and settled in Marlboro, and whose S., Benj'n, the immediate ancestor of Nathan, was one of the first settlers of Brookfield.

Rogers Chase, from Sutton, settled west and adjoining the Bartlett farm. His S. Royal is referred to pages 30, 31. Mr. Chase sold the south part of his farm and the buildings thereon; built on the north part; where he d. 1814, æ. 81. This place is now given up.

Joseph Stockwell, also from Sutton, was the purchaser of the south part of the Rogers Chase farm. He and his wife d. 1816, æ. 86. and 87. They brought up a large family; several of their children settled in town, from whom have sprung the numerous families of this name. Their S., Judah, settled at home: was succeeded by his S., Emmons, who m., Elvira, a sister of John Wood, Esq., and died in the prime of life. Their S., John W., is the present proprietor, with whom lives his widowed mother.

The place nearly south of this, is said to have been opened by one Putnam. It was bought by Capt. Sibley, who settled his son-in-law, Jonathan Pierce, upon it. He was succeeded by his S., Sibley, whose S., Sibley, responded to one of the Toasts at the Centennial dinner. Sibley sold to Columbus and John Pierce. the former a brother, and the latter a brother-in-law of Sibley Pierce. Columbus died, and John, who m. his sister, Susan, became sole proprietor. He is now living upon the place with his second wife, having m. Mrs. Charlotte Bryant, sister of his first wife, and mother of Rev. Albert Bryant, our Centennial Poet now a misssionary at Sivas, Turkey.

Lt. Edward Holman, from Sutton, settled nearly midway between Tarrant Cutler and Silas Jones, both of which places have already been illustrated. The cellar hole, on the west side of the road, marks the place of this sturdy old settler. He descended from a Welchman, who, with two brothers, all " impressed seamen" obtained a furlough from their ship to visit our shores, but never took the trouble to report themselves again to the Captain.

This may account for the gallantry of their race in our Revolution. Col. Holman, a Sutton man, commanded one of our Regiments,—our settler was a kinsman and served as Lt. under him,—and tradition in the family saith, that the British used to say, ' they had as lief see the Devil a-coming as Col. Holman on his gray mare.' The Lt. came here with nine children, of whom both sons and daughters had large families in town. At present, however, Seth N. Holman is left alone, among the men of the town, to bear up the name.

Thomas White, who m. Hannah Estabrook, sister of Joseph Estabrook, Esq., settled on a back road nearly east from Holman's. The family removed to West Boylston. Cyrus Holman, S. of John and grandson of Lt. Edward Holman bought the place. He was killed here while repairing the building; was succeeded by Luke Beals, who sold to Silas Bacheller, the present proprietor.

Benj. Clark, from Abington, settled at the end of a short road south of Silas Jones. He m. Mehitable Edson of Bridgewater; served two years in the war; was a " singing master;" d. 1815, æ. 66; his wife, 1841, æ. 88; was succeeded by his S., Benj., who m. Susannah Dolbear, of Templeton, and d. 1833, æ. 73. His widow, now in her 91st. year, lives with their S., Timothy, the present proprietor of this good farm. She attended the Centennial. Several other sons of Benj. Sen., settled in town,— Edson, who succeeded Benj. Blanchard, and still lives on that place. Eber who settled east of Tarrant Cutler's, and m. Sally, D., of David Chase. She still survives him and lives in Fitchburg, with her daughters; and Samuel, who m. Miss Ward, of Athol, and settled next north of the Dexter place.

Jon'n. Fiske, settled next south of Silas Jones'; was succeeded by Dea. Amos Jones, brother of Silas. He removed to Putney Vt. where he lately died. Dea. Jonas W. Turner S., of Jarathmal, is now proprietor of the place.

David Fiske, settled next south; sold to Col. Ebenezer Newel, from Brookfield, whose wife was Sarah Banister. They had 12 children. He was a Revolutionary Soldier; became a trader; removed from town and d. in Bethel, Me. æ. 89. Rev. Ebenezer F. Newel, a son, now in his 90th year, re-visited town in June last. Silas Hale Sen. bought this place, and settled his S.

Stephen upon it. He was succeeded by his S., John W. Hale, the present proprietor.

Josiah Waite, settled at the corner of the road south, where his great-grandson, Jesse F. Wheeler, now lives; d. 1835, æ. 89; was succeeded by his grandson, the late Col. Josiah Wheeler, and father of Jesse F.

Paul Wheeler, from Acton, m. Eunice, D., of Josiah Waite; settled east and upon a portion of Waite's land. Josiah Wheeler was his S., by his first wife, Eunice; by a second wife he had other children; among them, Leonard, the "Village Blacksmith" in the middle of the town, and Nelson, who m. Rebecca, D., of the late Hon. Rufus Bullock. He graduated at Yale, 1836; taught in Worcester; became Professor in Brown University; and d. 1855, æ. 42, at his father-in-law's. Mrs. Wheeler, and the two surviving sons, reside in Worcester.

Benj'n. Blanchard, settled still farther east; and owned a large tract of land, including most of what is now covered by So. Royalston Village, and on, nearly to Winchendon line. He was quite a mechanical character; invented a wheel with a register for measuring distances on the roads, and was often seen testing his wheel upon our highways. He built the first saw mill in So. Royalston, near where now stands S. S. Farrar's shop. Edson Clark succeeded him, and lives upon the fine site fronting the main street, but set back a little therefrom. His sons Ambrose and Lyman, live in the village, Ambrose next west of his father's.

Silas Hale, settled south of the village at the corner of the Templeton and Philipston roads. He and his wife, Lydia Stow, were from Stowe. The farm used to belong to Philipston; and has had a high reputation. The majestic elm, near the house, was set out by his S., Stephen, in 1790. He d. 1852, æ. 83; and was succeeded by his S., Silas. The place is now in the hands of Anon Stockwell, who m. one of the daughters of Silas

Hale Jr. Another D., m. Dr. Gould, for some years the physician of So. Royalston, who is now settled in Templeton.

Capt. Enoch Whitmore, from Acton, m. Sally, D., of Josiah Waite, and settled north of the Village, not far from schoolhouse, No. 9. He served seven years in the War. His D., Sally m. Timothy Lewis Esq. The captain, at length, removed to the Village and lived near his son-in-law; where he d. 1844, æ. 84. The old place was discontinued. His son-in-law was drowned in 1853, while attempting to rescue a child from the river. His widow still lives in the Village. Two of the sons are ministers, Joseph W., and Timothy Willard,—the latter superintendent of the Methodist Missions in the " Department of the South," with his residence in Charleston, S. C. Two other sons, John and Enoch T. reside in Athol.

The *White* and *Fisher* place, so called, above Capt. Whitmore's, and nearly opposite School House No. 9, was early owned if not settled, by Isaac Whitmore, who afterwards bought Moses Town's farm. He sold to Stephen, S. of Lt. Edward Holman. After the death of Stephen Holman, a Mr. White, and Cromwell Fisher bought the farm and it is still known as the White and Fisher place. Stephen Tolman's first settlement was at the corner of the road east of the school house. His S., Rev. Sidney Holman, was present and one of the Vice Presidents on Centennial day. He made a good speech at the table. Harriet, one of the daughters of Mr. Holman, m. Solyman Heywood, and still lives in town. The youngest S., Stephen, graduated at Williams College, 1839. Dea. Simeon Stockwell bought this place. He m. Ruth Piper, who, since his death, m. Elisha Childs, and still lives with him on the place.

Isaac Norcross, settled north of this last place; d. 1817, and was succeeded by his S., Dea. Joseph, who was succeeeded by his S., James Norcross, the present proprietor.

Josiah Piper, Jr., settled on this road, some distance north of Norcross; m. Molly, D. of Capt. Gad Pierce. He and his nephews, Capt. Jonas and Capt. George Pierce, are the three *teamsters*, referred to page 61. He built a second house on the place and settled his S., Luke, with him; d. 1837, æ. 70. His S., Luke, lately deceased, leaving the place to his S. Ch. J. Piper, the present proprietor.

Josiah Piper, Sen., settled south of school-house No. 9. m. a sister of Capt. Isaac Davis of Acton, who fell at the head of his men, in the *Battle of Concord*. His S., Isaac m. Jerusha Lyon, and lived in this neighborhood awhile, but ultimately removed from town.

Arba Sherwin, who lives south of this last named place, bought of Capt. Jonas Pierce. The place, as we understand, was first opened by Rufus Forbush, who sold to William, father of Capt. Jonas. Capt. Jonas afterwards bought the Lt. Allen place; sold to Obadiah W. Goddard, and bought of his brother, Capt. George Pierce, the place now owned by Barnet Bullock, Esq., formerly the John and then the Dea. Seth Holman place.

Isaac Gale, S. of the original settler of this name, settled on the road that turns west, a little below the Sherwin place. He m. Elizabeth, d. of Jonathan Cutler; and was succeeded by his S. Otis, who lately died. The place now owned by O. Percival Gale.

Isaac Gale, S. of the Isaac above named, settled near the corner of the road that turns east, still farther below Sherwin's. He m. Rhoda, D. of Capt. Joseph Jacobs. He has settled his S., O. Hartwell, with him.

Asa Turner, from Grafton, settled on this road next beyond Gale's. His S. Jarathmal, succeeded him. He m. Jerusha D., of Joseph Manning, and died upon this place.

Joseph Manning, settled the next place upon this road. His D. Susannah, m. Dea. Lemuel Newton, of Phillipston, who died a few years ago, and she now lives in So. Royalston. Abel Manning, merchant of Fitchburg, was born on this place.

Dea. Isaac Stockwell, m. Melinda, D., of Asa Turner, and bought the Manning, and part of the Forbush farms. His S.,

Elmond now lives upon this place; his S., Edmond resides in the village of So. Royalston, and is proprietor in the paint, and brush wood shops there; while Anon, another S., who m. a D., of Silas Hale, resides near the Hale farm, of which he is now the proprietor.

David Forbush, settled the last farm on this road, within the bounds of Royalston. He was succeeded by his S., Heman, who still resides on the place; as does also Betsy Forbush, D., of David, now in her 86th. year.

Dea. Isaac Esty, settled the first place west of the common, near the foot of Jacob's hill, so called. He was one of the eight persons who " embodied " with the 1st Baptist Church of Royalston, 1768, and became its first deacon: was a man of considerable property and a highly respected citizen. His aged Mother came to town with him: rode in a chaise, which it required several men to steady and help over the obstructions of the way. She was the first adult female that died in Royalston. Dea. Jacob Esty succeeded his father upon the farm and in the deaconship. He m. Sarah. D. of Simeon Chamberlain; d. 1829 æ. 86, his wife, the same year, æ. 80. He was succeeded by Capt. Joseph Jacobs, from Athol, who m. Sarah Bragg, and who, planted the avenue of maples that adorn the hill, and shade the road above this ancient house. After his death the place was held by the family; but has now lately been sold by John W. Green, who m. Olive, D., of Capt. Jacobs. Neither the Esty, nor the Captain's name is now upheld in town, by their descendants; but the *Jacobs' Hill* remains a fixture among us; and the long lines of maples flourish and mark the landscape from afar.

Asa Jones, settled S. W., of this place, on the borders of Long Pond. The farm is now a pasture, and the buildings gone. He was the first Scribe of the Baptist Ch. One of his sons became an eminent Baptist minister.

Simeon Chamberlain, from Sutton, settled next north of Esty's. His house stood in the barn-lot, and not far from the barn, as the buildings are now arranged. He "embodied" with the Baptist Church in 1768; was the first male teacher that drew pay from the town, receiving an order for 18 shillings, "for two weeks schooling" in 1769. His D., Mary, drew 4s. 9d. 2qrs. "for keeping school two weeks," the same year. He d. 1779, æ. 77: was succeeded by his S., John, who was thrice married, 1st to Mary Elliot; 2d, to Hannah Pratt; and 3d. to the Widow Holden, whose S., John Holden, succeeded to the place. He sold to his brother, Jonathan, the present proprietor. The house now stands on the east side of the road, not far from the corner.

Capt. Pelatiah Metcalf, from Wrentham, settled next north; m. Lydia, D., of Dea. Isaac Esty; built a saw-mill on the site of the mill now owned by Nathaniel Greely: established a potash: was an active business man, and a prominent citizen. He d. suddenly, 1807, æ. 62. His S., Capt. Isaac, succeeded him; sold to his brother, Jacob, who lately died upon the place, which since, has been sold to Horatio Brewer, the present proprietor. Enoch, another S., settled farther north. His S., C. B. Metcalf, A. M. is Principal of the "Highland School," Worcester. Another S., Isaac N. is "Teacher of Vocal and Instrumental Music," in the same school. Dr. Pelatiah Metcalf, S., of Capt. Pelatiah, lives in Woonsocket, R. I. in his 81st year.

Michael Grant, settled next north. The first person, whose death appears on the Records, was his S., Stephen, who was buried "amid the pines under the hill." Grant sold to Obadiah Walker Jr. He was succeeded by his S., Asa, who m. Austis, D., Capt. Joseph Jacobs, and d. 1860, æ. 82. His widow, and S., Joseph, still live in town. The place has lately been sold out of the family.

Aaron Grant, settled next north, was a good farmer; persisted in wearing "small clothes," dispensing with the long stockings, knee-buckles, and shoes, through all but the winter months. He m. for his second wife, widow Sarah Morse, D. of Capt. Jonas Parker, of Lexington and Revolutionary memory. Her sister Betsey, m. Michael Perry, whose D. Betsey, m. Samuel Morse, the present proprietor of the Dea. Bacheller place, and whose D. is the wife of Wm. H. Emerson. Grant was succeeded by his S., Aaron, whose widow, and S., Aaron, held the place some years after his death. They now live upon the common, and the place is owned by Lyman Carroll.

Henry Goddard, from Athol, settled north; sold to his brother. Nahum Goddard, who m. Sally, D., of William Pierce. He sold to his son-in-law, Capt. Cyrus B. Reed, the present proprietor. His S., Sandford, and his S. from Orange, Hon. Davis Goddard, were present at the Centennial,—the latter as a Vice President.

Squier Davis, S., of Lt. John Davis, settled next north; settled his S. John upon the place, and removed to the Fuller place. He afterwards lived and died with his S., Joseph, dying 1854, æ. 92. John sold to Hon. George Whitney and removed to the west, where he soon after died. The place is now owned by Cyrus P. and William G. Reed, sons of Capt. C. B. Reed; having been carried on for the several years past by the first named proprietor.

Stephen Raymond, S. of Edward. settled next north; m. Rhoda, sister of Joseph Estabrook, Esq.; brought up his family upon place, and died here; was succeeded by his S., James; he sold to Sandford Goddard; removed to Keene, but now resides in Brooklyn, N. Y. He was present and one of the Vice Presidents, on Centennial occasion. His brother Joseph Raymond, Esq., residing upon the common, is the only member of Stephen Raymond's family, now in town.

Joseph Davis, S. of Squier, is the proprietor of the next place, now including most of the Raymond farm. Mr. Davis is one of our largest land holders, and is still a hale and laborious farmer. Enoch Metcalf formerly owned the original place, which had, perhaps, been already opened previously to his purchase.

James Forbes, formerly McForbes, settled next north, and at the extremity of this long range of high and good land rising from the Tully, and confronting the equally elevated range on the opposite, or western side of the river,—from its excellence, as pasture land, called Goshen. James Forbes was succeeded by his S., James, who sold to his S. John, who died in the late war. Joseph Davis now owns this farm.

Ebenezer Blanding, after settling a place near "the city," so called, opened a farm, N. W. from the last place, and near the point where the road, after crossing the Tully and ascending the opposite hill, turns to the north. He sold to Calvin Forbes, S. of James Sen. Forbes is dead, and his family have all left town; but his name still adheres to this locality and the "Falls" west of his house, notwithstanding Professor Hitchcock proposed another and more characteristic name.—*Royal Cascade.*

Joseph Hix, or Hicks, as now written, settled next north; he soon sold to the father of the present proprietor, Luther Ballou. The latter m. a daughter of Capt. Joseph Davis; brought up 12 children, all of whom have settled out of town; and now he and his wife have closed their house, and are, for the present residing with some of their children in Winchendon. It is rumored, however, that this fine old place is to be fitted up as a Summer Retreat for those who seek country life. rejuvenation, relaxation, or healthful pleasure during the *heated term* of the year. It is a splendid place for such an enterprise; accessible from the Cheshire R. R.; in the immediate neighborhood of the Royal Cascade, and environed by wild and romantic country scenery. Suitable buildings, properly appointed and kept, would doubtless secure an ample patronage. Large numbers, even now, without attractions other, than those that nature furnishes, annually visit this interesting locality. We hope the "rumor" may speedily pass into a consummated fact.

Hicks, after selling this place, bought of one Stockwell a new settlement between the Forbes' hills north of the road, a short distance back of which and upon the Tully, he put up a grist and saw mill. These are now dismantled; and the place deserted.

Returning to Capt. Metcalf's place, and passing west, by the road, part of the way still open, and then through the fields, woodland and pastures to the S. W., we come to the site of *Thomas Chamberlain*, from Sutton, and brother of Simeon. His buildings were on the first *hard land*, north of Long Pond, and between the Tully and the Saw-mill brook, so called. His wife, Charity, and his S., Thomas, " embodied " with the Baptist Ch. In this family the town boarded the first person requiring public aid. The original settler and his wife died upon this place, and were buried in the grave-yard near by. They were succeeded by their S., Thomas, who however, did not long remain. The place has long been given up.

Elisha Rich, supposed also to have come from Sutton, settled about half a mile north of the last named place. His house stood east of the Tully, opposite the first bridge north of Long Pond. He is referred to on page 42. The Proprietors, in 1771 gave him the title to " settlers lot " 27. containing 200 acres, "he having settled two families thereon, and in all respects done and performed the duty of two settlers on said lot." He also owned a lot, bordering on the N. W. corner of Pierpont's Grant, and adjoining the State line. Mr Rich, early removed from town, laboring in several places, and gathering and leading Baptist churches, until at length, he was ordained, Oct. 5th, 1774, by the church in Chelmsford, being, according to Barker's History, the first Baptist Church organized in Middlesex Co. The house of Elder Rich, after some years, was occupied by Uzziah Green as a tavern. It was in this immediate vicinity, on the west side of the Tully, that the first Baptist meeting house in town was built. It is referred to on pages 41, 42; and there was here, so to speak, the second center of the town—with its meeting house, tavern and burial lot. But after the union of the Baptists of Royalston and Warwick, and the building of their new house of worship, in the west part of the town, this once populated and pleasant neighborhood, went to decay, the old road was given up, these ancient buildings one by one disappeared, and at length the burying ground of the fathers was lost to sight, and almost to memory, amid the usurping forest.

Returning north to the now travelled road, and passing west, we come to the settlement of *Joshua Dean*, now the property of Dexter Underwood. He built west of the present site upon the old road; became quite wealthy; and at length removed to New York state with his S., Joshua. His S., Jeremiah, built the saw mill, now enlarged and fitted up with modern machinery. His D. Hannah, m. Benj. Perry. She resided in town till recently, and her D. Flora, m. Joseph L. Perkins, who resides upon the homestead of his father, Rev. Ebenezer Perkins.

Andrew Kendall, Esq., settled the next place west; but sold and removed to the Peleg Kingsley place, west of the old Baptist common, where he died. James Walker, S. of Elijah, bought the Kendall farm; m. Sally, D. of Jonas Brewer, Sen., and lately died upon the place. His widow, now 86, was present at the Centennial, and resides with her S. Moses Walker, the present proprietor.

Russell Wheeler, widely known as Dr. Wheeler, from his extensive practice as a veterinarian, settled next west of Walker's. He lost 5 children by the prevalent epidemic in 1795,—all he then had. He himself d. 1825, aged 59.; was succeeded by his S. Capt. Russell Wheeler; who sold to his brother Benj., the present proprietor. His house was burned in 1852, and has not been rebuilt. He now resides in So. Royalston; his farm being mainly turned out to pasturage.

Silvanus Bliss, from Rehoboth, settled next west of Wheeler: was active in bringing about the union of the Baptists in Royalston and Warwick, and in obtaining the Act of incorporation in 1807. He removed from town, and was succeeded by Abel Bliss, S. of Nathan, and father of the Nathan Bliss who is the present occupant; and also of Harrison Bliss, of Worcester, one of our Vice Presidents on Centennial Day.

Nathan Bliss, brother of Silvanus, settled next west. He was in the Revolutionary War; d. 1852, æ. 90; his wife, 1862, æ. 97. The house is now tenantless.

West of this is "the city," so called. Here were built, in 1802, two public houses of considerable pretensions for those days, one of them had a store attached. Capt. Peleg Kingsley built one of these houses, now the dwelling house of Gardner and Moses Garfield; and Asahel Davis, the other; now supplanted by the new residence of Benj. Buffum. Here, too, stands the third meeting house of the Baptist Church, and school house, No. 3; all of which may justify the old familiar designation of this neighborhood,—"the city."

Lewis Horton, the first settler west of the Tully, located north of where the present Baptist meeting house stands. He was from Rehoboth, and died young. The old road by his settlement has been *turned*, and the buildings are gone.

Ebenezer Blanding, also from Rehoboth, settled north of this place; sold to his brother, Shubel, and settled the Calvin Forbes' farm, so called. Shubel m. the widow of Horton, and annexed his farm to his own,—now known as the Graves' place. He out-lived three wives, and d. 1832, æ 81. His S., Shubel, became a physician, settled in South Carolina, and died shortly before the out-break of the late Rebellion, being at the time of his death, a citizen of Charleston.

Eliphalet Rogers, a lineal descendant, in the fourth or fifth generation, of the martyr, John Rogers; bought a place, newly begun by one Drake, and settled next north of Blanding's. He was thrice married, and had a large family of children.

Dea. Moulton Bullock, from Rehoboth, took up the place next north. Came into town before the Revolution; was a highly respected citizen, and for many years Dea. of the Baptist Ch.; d. 1818, æ. 75; his wife, Oct. 11, 1806. This place is now owned by Horace, S. of Jason Fisher.

Hugh Bullock, came in during the Revolution, and settled north of his brother Moulton, where he lived till his sons grew up, left the farm and engaged in other business, when he built on the common west of his S. Barnet's house, where Ch. H. Newton now lives; and died there 1837, æ. 85. His wife Rebecca d. 1809, æ. 50. Hugh Bullock was one of the company that started for Saratoga, to repel the invasion of Burgoyne. Of the children of this family, Rufus, Moulton, Calvin, Barnet and Candice, only the two last survive.

Lt. John Davis, Samuel Fuller, and Lt. John Foster, all from Rehoboth, removed to town in 1778, each with a family of eight children, and settled in this part of the town. *Davis* next north of Hugh Bullock, *Fuller* north of Davis, and *Foster* on the farm now owned by Rev. Silas Kenney. Fuller and Foster ultimately removed from town. Davis remained. Eleven of his children had families of their own, several of whom settled in town. His sons, Squier, John, Jr., and Sylvester, served in the war. John Davis d. 1794, æ. 58; and is represented by all of that name in town. His wife d. 1832, æ. 92.

Ebenezer Ingalls, settled east of the grave yard, in this section. The road used to run by his farm; but is now changed and the farm given up.

Christopher, Ebenezer, Nathan and David Bullock, cousins of Dea. Moulton, and Hugh Bullock, bought of the Prop's, about 1770, lots 77, 79, and 80, containing 345 1-2 acres, at 8s per acre. These lots lay in the extreme N. W. corner of the town, covering the modern farms of Martin Hardy, Adriel White, and the late Capt. Joseph Bliss. They were all stalwart men,—David the tallest man in town. Their tarry was not very long; for when they had their places well opened, and before they had yet lost the vigor of manhood, like one of Irving's characters, they shouldered their axes, and were off again for a new country; taking York State in their way.

David Fisher, from Attleboro' settled south of this purchase, and adjoining the late Capt. Bliss place. He was a man of strong mind, somewhat eccentric, but a good school master. An earnest opponent of the old law, requiring every one to pay for the support of religious worship,—he became a leader of the "Free Donation Society," referred to page 44; after the repeal of that law he became a regular contributor in sustaining the institutions of the Gospel. He d. 1850, æ. 87; his wife the year following, æ. 86. Their S., Jason, now occupies the place.

The next place south is now occupied by *Rev. Silas Kenney*, a native of Sutton, and formerly pastor of the 1st. Baptist Church, and a highly respectable citizen, referred to page 41. This place, opened at first by Lt. John Foster, has been occupied by several Baptist clergymen, before the Rev. Mr. Kenney became its proprietor.

Daniel Peck, from Rehoboth, first settled where Harvey W. Bliss now lives; but subsequently exchanged with Timothy Bliss, Jr., for the place where Dea. Ebenezer Pierce lately died. Here he d. 1814, æ. 73, and his wife, 1832, æ. 77. They had 9 children, and have been numerously, and are still represented in town by descendants.

John Peck, settled on the S. E. corner of the roads that intersect, a short distance south of his brother Daniel's first settlement. He was author of a Poem on Universalism, which passed through several editions, and has lately, with some other pieces, been reproduced by John P. Jewett, & Co. Boston, and H. P. B. Jewett, Cleveland, O. When his large family had grown up, he removed with them to Vermont. Stephen Gates succeeded him; and the place is now occupied by his S., Whitman Gates.

The meeting house, built by the united Baptist churches and societies of Royalston and Warwick, stood on the open space at the N. W. corner of these intersecting roads; referred to page 42, hence, the still popular designation of this locality,—"the old Baptist common."

Peleg Kingsley, from Rehoboth, first settled the place west of this common, on the Warwick road, where Daniel Peck died. He was one of the earliest settlers in this part of the town: was a blacksmith; brought up a large family. It was his S. Capt. Peleg Kingsley, who built one of the public houses at *the city*, already mentioned. This family is not now represented in town. Timothy Bliss, Jr., followed on this place; he was succeeded by Daniel Peck. After him came Andrew Kendall, Esq. formerly proprietor of the Moses Walker place. He was succeeded by Dea. Ebenezer Pierce, who d. 1863, æ. 68. This farm has lately been purchased by a Mr. Whitney.

Timothy Bliss, from Rehobath, settled opposite of the last named farm, a short distance south of the road. He raised up a large family, and settled his S., Isreal, with him on the homestead where he also had a family of 11 children. This last family removed to New York State; and the place became incorporate with other farms. The buildings are now gone. The original proprietor, when he first came to town, made a purchase of 600 acres, which must have covered a part of the Moore Grant. He d. 1822, æ. 89. His S., Timothy, m. Tammy Waite, and settled at first opposite his father's on the place last named, which he afterwards exchanged, as has been stated, with Daniel Peck. On his last place he was succeeded by his S., Daniel, who m, Harriet, D., of Lt. Daniel Peck; d. 1863, æ. 66; and was succeeded by his S., Harvey W. Aaron Bliss, S., of the original settler, m. Molly Woodbury; bought the Peleg Jennings farm, south of the Baptist Common; brought up a family there, and d. 1849, æ. 96. His S., Benj'n. W, Bliss, is the present proprietor.

Abiel Briggs, about 1770, bought of the Prop's. the 200 acres, originally a part of the Moore Grant, and of which mention is made on p. 28. His farm lay south, and adjoining, the last named. He sold to Ebenezer Bullock; who sold to Lt. Daniel Peck, S., of Daniel already illustrated. Lt. Peck m. Dilly, D.. of Isaac Gale, Sen.; had a family of 4 sons and 9 daughters, several of whom settled in town. His S., Sullivan succeeded him on the place, and still owns it. His D., Harriet, m. Daniel Bliss, and still lives with her S., Harvey W. Bliss. His son Lyman, settled south of "the city," where his S., Philander, now lives. Another D., Delia, m. Capt. George Peirce, who resides upon the common in the middle of the town. Chauncy, S., of Lt. Peck, residing in Boston, was one of the Vice Presidents on the day of our late Anniversary.

Jonathan Gale, brother-in-law of Lt. Peck, m. Rhoda Baker, and settled next south, of the Peck place. His farm adjoined Warwick on the west, and Orange on the south. He was a Revolutionary Soldier, m. for his second wife, Susannah Matthews, who still lives near the old Baptist common, and draws a pension by virtue of her husband's services. This place is now the property of Hiram Harrington, whose wife is a grand-daughter of Nathan Cutting, one of the first settlers, Isaac Gale, S., of Jon'n, m. Tamah, D., of Sam'l. Goddard, and died on the Matthew's place. The family have now all removed from town. S. C. Gale Esq. of Minneapolis, Minnesota, and Rev. Amory Gale, were of this family.

Nathan Goddard, from Shrewsbury, bought a large tract south of the Gale place; built a public house, tannery and saw mill and carried on an extensive business. From the incorporation of Royalston, till this S. W. corner of the town was set off to form a part of Orange, Mr. Goddard was an active and respected citizen here. He m. Dorothy Stevens of Petersham, and d. 1806, æ. 81.

Returning to the Baptist common, and taking the road to the middle of the town, we come to the place opened by *Lt. Samuel Goddard*, from Sutton. He built a tannery on the stream west of his house, which has been quite an extensive establishment; but is now discontinued, and the buildings mostly gone. He brought up a family of 10 children, and d. 1808, æ. 64; was succeeded by his S., Salmon, who continued and enlarged his father's business; became Colonel, Esquire and Deacon ; honored all his public offices, and died highly respected, at the age of 58. His S., Salmon, now occupies the place.

Jonas Brewer, from Shrewsbury, settled next east. His parents came to town, and lived with him. The father, William, d. 1796, æ. 90; the mother, 1800, æ. 90. Jonas m. Elizabeth Garfield; brought up a family of 8 or 9 children; d. 1817, æ. 65; his widow m. Dea. Ammi Falkner, and d. 1838, æ. 86. The original settler was succeeded by his S., Jonas, who has settled his S., Lewis, with him. Another S., Horatio, now owns the Capt. Pelatiah Metcalf place.

Jonathan Matthews, from Rehoboth, settled on the road leading south from the Brewer farm. He died, leaving a widow, his aged mother, Mrs. Susannah Carpenter,—named on p. 61,—and three daughters, Susannah, Hannah, and Lucy, and but small means for their support. Mrs. Carpenter out-lived her daughter-in-law, and died at the age of 105, mainly supported, and tenderly cared for, to the last, by her grand-daughters. They now live together in a house adjoining the Baptist common, all well stricken in years, but held in remembrance for their filial duty to their aged and dependant grandmother.

Joshua Garfield, from Shrewsbury, bought of one Wells, who had lately opened the next place on this road. Here he brought up a large family of children; and was succeeded by his S., Moses; whose sons, Gardner and Moses, live at "the city."

Solomon Peck, brother of John and Daniel, settled at the end of this road; brought up a family of 13 children; was succeeded by his S., Benoni, Peck Esq. Here he, too, brought up a family of 10 children, who successively settled out of town; and now, lately, the Esquire himself has removed to Fitzwilliam, N. H., leaving this once populous road entirely deserted. Esq. Peck was Lt. in the company called out from Royalston, for the defence of Boston, in the last war with England, and afterwards commanded the company. He was much engaged in Justice and Probate business and his antiquarian researches have been of great service in the preparation of this Memorial of his native town.

Returning to the Brewer place, from thence east to "the city," and on the Athol road south, we come to the farm settled, at first, by one Harris, sold by him to Cyrus Bassett, who established, and for some time carried on, a tannery here and died upon the place. It is now the property of *Jarvis Davis Esq.* S., of Capt. Joseph Davis, who was S., of Lt. John Davis. Esq. Davis has recently settled with him, his son-in-law, Adriel C. S., of Adriel White.

Jonathon Bosworth, settled the place next south. He was ancestor of all the Bosworths in town; d. 1801, æ. 88; was succeeded by his S., Ichabod. The place, after passing through the hands of several other proprietors, became the property, and is now occupied by Marshall Herrick,

Ephraim Hill, and *Elijah Walker*, who received their farms from Jonah Hill, father of Ephraim, and father-in-law of Walker, lived on a road that turns to the west from the Athol road, a little south from the last named place. Hill m. a sister of Walker. He d. 1826, æ. 65; his wife 1841, æ. 80; leaving one son and five daughters. The place is now owned by Elijah Walker, a grandson of the Walker who first settled the adjoining farm. Walker who m. Abigail Hill, was succeeded by his S., Willard, whose widow m. Israel Lamb, who succeeded Willard Walker on the place. He has now settled Geo. O. Richardson on his farm. He m. a D., of Willard Walker; and is the S., of the present Mrs. Benoni Peck Esq., formerly Mrs. Melinda Richardson, the second wife of Abijah Richardson.

Elisha White, from Orange, settled on the Lemuel Whitney place, about a half mile south of Walker's. White raised up a large family here; d. 1811, æ. 58; his widow married again and d. 1850, æ. 94. Adriel White, who lives on a farm within the purchase of David Bullock and brothers, is a S., of Elisha White;

and has lately settled his S., Asaph. with him. The Elisha White place is now deserted.

John Stockwell, and *John Turner*, had each a farm east of the Hill and Walker farms; but they are gone and their places merged in other farms.

Daniel Warren, settled the farm on the Athol road, next south of this side road. He sold to Capt. Joseph Davis, father of Jarvis Davis Esq. who d. here; and was succeeded by Lyman Peck, lately deceased. The place is now owned by Philander S., of Lyman Peck.

Daniel Warren, also opened the next place south; which afterwards came into the possession of a Mr. Pratt, and is still owned by Daniel Pratt, a resident of Petersham.

Paul Ellis, a School Teacher, and licensed Baptist preacher commenced a place next south; sold to *Levi Thurston*, who afterwards was a deacon in the Cong'l Church, and died on the place, at an advanced age. The place is now given up.

Elnathan Jacobs, S., of Elder Whitman Jacobs, settled and erected the buildings still standing on the road that turns to the east, just south of the Thurston place; sold to Timothy Whitney; and Whitney to Capt. Asahel Davis, S., of Lt. John Davis, and father of Cyrus, and Daniel. He m. Deborah Mason; and d. here 1859 æ. 84; his wife, 1860 æ. 81. He built one of the public houses in "the city." His S., Daniel is the present proprietor of this place.

Asa Clark, settled next south on the Athol road; now owned by Dea. Francis Jacobs, S., of Dea. Thomas Jacobs.

Ebenezer Elliot, S., of the Elliot who originally settled on the common, opened a farm a little west of the road, next south; sold to Elder Moses Kenny, who d. here 1800, æ. 47. He was succeeded upon the place by Dea. Thomas Jacobs, S., of Elder Whitman Jabobs; d. 1849, æ. 69, and was succeeded by his S., Whitman, the present proprietor.

Uzziah Green, S., of Nahum, of Revolutionary memory, settled next south; sold to Elder Simeon Jacobs, and opened a tavern on the place formerly owned by Elisha Rich. Elder Jacobs was succeeded by his S., Simeon, who died leaving a family of 9 sons, the eldest but 17. Several of these sons settled abroad and prospered in life, some as professional men and some as merchants. This place, now furnished with good buildings, is the property of Cyrus Davis, one of our prominent and active citizens.

The site of David Chase's first settlement was south of this place, on the east side of the road, and a short distance north of school house No. 8. His house was burned, and he removed and settled with his father, Lt. Francis Chase.

Jon'n. Shepardson, from Templeton, settled next south; left his place to his S. John, who sold to David Cook, and Son. David Cook, the father, d. 1844, æ. 91. He drew the pension of an orderly Sergeant. David Cook, Jr., died the same year, and left the place to his S. Caleb A. Cook, Esq., who recently sold to Rev. Lorenzo Tandy, pastor of the Baptist Church.

Daniel Shepardson, S. of Jon'n. settled the next place south. He d. 1856, æ. 80; his wife, 1850, æ. 78. They had 7 children. Rev. Daniel Shepardson, of Cincinnati, O., and Rev. John Shepardson of Petersham being of the number. Their S. Eri, now owns the place.

Isaac Shepardson, also S. of Jon'n, settled next south, nearly opposite the residence of Luke Bemis. This place is now known as the Ruggles' place.

Joshua Doane, from Cape Cod, settled next south; and brought up a family of children on the place, of whom a S., Amos, and a D, the wife of Joel O. Flagg, have families in town. He died at his son's, Simeon Doane, in the N. E. part of the town; and the place was bought by Samuel, S. of Benj. Clark. He d. 1858, æ. 65. His widow lives here with C. C. Chapin, who m. her daughter. This farm now has new and good buildings, finely located.

Barney Paine, from Athol opened the next and last early settlement on this road, within our limits; built a saw mill on the Tully south of his house; sold to Lemuel Whitney, and he to Ebenezer W. Dexter, who m. Cynthia, D. of Moses Walker, rebuilt the saw mill and erected the present handsome residence. Mr. Dexter d. suddenly 1860, æ. 80. His widow lives upon the place with her S. Bela.

Reuben Putnam, settled on the place now owned by Stephen A. Burbank; sold to James Dexter from Grafton, father of Ebenezer, who, when advanced in life, sold to John Burbank from Oakham, and removed to his son's, where he died. John Burbank was succeeded by his S. Stephen A., the present proprietor. Rev. Perry Burbank, S. of John, now resides in Sutton.

Aaron Putnam, and a Mr. Brown, had early and neighboring habitations westwardly from Burbank's. They both sold out to Moses Walker, from Athol, about 1790. Mr. Walker, m. Lydia Bigelow, of Sutton. He left his place to his S., John B. lately deceased. The widow of Moses died upon this place 1864, æ. 93. The widow of John B. and the family now reside in Keene, N. H.

The old road continued on north by the Walker place on the west side, and at no great distance from the Tully and Long Pond, to the first Baptist meeting house, and thence into the Royalston and Warwick road. Along this old road were several early families, and among them those of Michael, and Enos Metcalf, brothers of Captain Peletiah Metcalf. Enos m. a D. of Elder Whitman Jacobs; and was long a Deacon in the Baptist Church. Daniel Mosman lived in this vicinity, near the north end of Long Pond. He removed from town, and the house was burned in 1814. His S. Daniel, returned from Wilmington, Vt. and m. Betsey Metcalf. Another S. born here, is a retired merchant in Boston.

Since the above was in the hands of the printer, we have ascertained the location of two or three more early settlers. *Samuel W. Bowker*, S. of Silas, settled on the Amos Jones place, north of Silas Cutting's. *Jon'n Hutchinson* succeeded Reuben Walker on what is now the F. H. Goddard place.—He owned the land still farther east, and sold off to William Brown, who established what is now the Prouty place.

John Whitmore settled in the vicinity of Capt. Enoch, and Whitmore. His house stood near the corner of the roads east from school house, No. 9. His S., Capt. John Whitmore, lives in So. Royalston.

The principal names, found upon our records, whose settlements and history we have no means of illustrating, are the following:—Elisha and Asa Clark, Moses McClellan, Simon Newton, Daniel and William Dike, Thomas Harrington, Moses Huse, Solomon Babcock, Daniel Brown, Lt. Samuel Marsh, Simeon Moory, Chester Morse, ——— Manly, Israel Cole, William Gilchrist, Daniel Owen, Ezra Pratt, Nath'l. Potter, Jonas Livermore, Lt. Micah French, Bartholemew French, John Chaplin, Thomas Norton, Peter Hadley, John Hazeltine, William Crawford. Dexter May, Phillip Sweetzer, Esq., Benj. Hardy, Oliver Warren, Nathan Wilder, Charles Whitney, Silvanus Ward, Joshua Heues, Jacob Sargent.

It has been difficult to abstain from introducing families who have come to town since 1800, and especially some of the very early families of this class; but it seemed necessary to restrict ourselves. As it is, this Note has far outrun our original intentions, and we fear it has gone equally beyond the patience of our readers.

We have often found ourselves at fault, after having, as we supposed, correctly illustrated a name or a localitiy, and been obliged to recast our work. We have labored to make the note as accurate as possible, and as full as we dared to make it. But after all it will doubtless need revision; and we would respectfully suggest to our readers, interested in these matters, and able to contribute to the correction and perfection of this work, to note errors, or deficiencies, in these illustrations, and take the trouble to make record of the same. Such notes, may be of great importance to the future historian of Royalston. This Committee volunteer their services, so long as it may be practicable for them, or either of them, to do so, to receive and put in a form for preservation, any *errata* or *supplementary matter*, that may promise to subserve the general purpose of this memorial volume in general, or this Note in particular.

NOTE J.—PAGE 36.   RELIGIOUS SOCIETIES.

Our original plan embraced a full note on our ecclesiastical History; but we find ourselves obliged either to give up this intention, forego the illustration of several topics which seem to demand a place in this memorial, or greatly exceed the limits beyond which we have not thought to go. We prefer the first alternative; and the rather, both because the *general sketch* of our religious organizations, presented in the address, gives appropriate relative prominence to this topic, and because this topic is more secure of public elucidation by the parties more immediately interested in the several denominations, than are most of the other matters of our common history.

Since the Address passed through the press we have been pointed to a single statement, in the *general sketch* therein given of the religious societies of Royalston, that is liable to convey a wrong impression. On page 44, the Union Society, organized in 1839, is spoken of as formed "out of a branch of the Baptist church in the west, and *some Universalists of Athol*." Most, if not all, of those who composed the second party to that union, were citizens of Royalston.

NOTE K.—PAGE 40.   HON. RUFUS BULLOCK.

A memorial of Royalston without some special notice of this distinguished citizen would manifestly be incomplete. He deserves commemoration not less for his personal influence and worth, while living, than for those liberal legacies, by which, dying, he sought to befriend his native town.

It is to be regretted that he who commemorated his coevals and associates, was forbidden, by the circumstances of the case, to perform the same office for Rufus Bullock himself.—In the absence of what would have been so much more desirable, we insert the folllowing notice of our common benefactor.

Hon. Rufus Bullock, eldest son of Hugh and Rebecca Bullock, was born in Royalston, Mass., Sept. 23, 1779; spent all his days in the town of his nativity; and here died, Jan. 10, 1858, æ. 78.

With small means he early laid the foundations of a good education, and became an acceptable school teacher before reaching his majority. He made this his business, in winter, for some years; "working out," mainly at farming, during the other seasons. Two or three of his schools in Truro, on the Cape, extended through most of the year. From school teaching he turned his attention to trade, attending store, as clerk, till he was induced to open a store on the common, on his own account. The encouragement was such, that he concluded to settle down in life as a country merchant, at first, in a small way, but with principles, and in a spirit, that had in them the promise already of that industry and thrift which terminated only with his long and prosperous life.

May 4th, 1808, he married Miss Sarah Davis, of Rindge, N. H. She still survives, and lives among us, the same industrious and cheerful matron, of the olden type, whose wisdom and energy helped to build the house; and who is still spared to enjoy it, when builded, and still to attract the children and children's children to the ancient homestead.

Mr. Bullock made it a rule, to expand his business as his means increased, never going beyond, but always occupying fully all his resources; and charging himself with the details, no less than the general management of his affairs. And so regular, and for a time so gradual, was his expansion, and so thoroughly did he train himself to a simple and systematic method, that he never lost the ability, as he never gave up the habit, of doing so, even when his business became various and heavy. Indeed he seemed to find recreation in its variety, and both refreshment and power by turning from one branch to another in his daily routine. He kept up his interest in farming, and was often in the field, not as a spectator, or intermedler, but a hearty laborer; and, while thus employed in the open air, gaining tone and vigor from manual exercise, or at a later period, while riding leisurely in his buggy to and from his factory in So. Royalston, he performed a vast deal of head-work, and saved a vast deal of office-work. Few business men have been less dependant upon clerks, and voluminous accounts and documents. His *mind* was his office; and it was not only portable, but to be trusted, both with extended details and general results.

He engaged personally in manufacturing about 1825; and soon made this his specialty, and by means of which, in an establishment, not large, but well conducted, he built up a large and solid fortune, and became widely known as a man of established and growing wealth, of eminent business talents, of high moral worth, and of a freshness and vigor, which scarcely age itself could invade. While others, of more pretensions, went down in the recurring financial reverses, he had always at command reserved resources for biding the times, and, in the end, of legitimately advancing his fortunes.

Mr. Bullock was not unknown in public life. Five years he represented the town in the General Court; two terms he served as Senator; was delegate to the Constitutional Conventions of 1820, and 1852; and was once chosen as a Presidential Elector.

He served the town in various offices, as his other business allowed; and brought to the discharge of all public trusts the same maxims and principles, as those by which he conducted his own private affairs.

In politics he was no changeling, in morals and religion no latitudinarian, though catholic, and without bigotry. His reading was select, and of the deepest and broadest thinkers. He retained with much accuracy, and quoted with aptness, both sentiments and language, which had approved themselves to his judgment, gratified his taste, or touched his heart. He reverenced the Bible, and studied it deeply, and with growing interest. He loved the old doctrines, and read the old divines, who, as he believed, most profoundly entered into the spirit, and most honestly interpreted and enforced the word of God.

He was an interesting companion, alike for his intelligence, and the practical and weighty views he had matured on the most important matters, not only of business, but of life. He was a good listener, and a fair and honest man in comparing views, and debating questions of difference in opinions or practice.

He was a patriot of the early type,—a gentleman of the olden school— a friend to be trusted, and a man whose principles bore the test of intimate acquaintance and inspection, and whose influence, unobtrusive, but potent, has been eminently useful.

While living he was a cheerful and liberal supporter of the institutions of learning and religion,—though in these, as in every thing else, he counseled economy and frugality,—dying, he left the material means, which, if wisely employed, will aid yet more, and more widely, in the support of our schools, and our churches.

We insert the clauses of his will, in which our schools and religious Societies, were remembered by him.

"*Thirteenth,* I give and bequeath to the first Congregational Society in the center of the town of Royalston, being the same with which I now worship, the sum of Five Thousand Dollars ($5000,) to be held and applied as follows; the interest of said Five Thousand Dollars shall be forever paid and applied annually or semi-annually for the support of preaching in said society; and it is my will that a Committee, chosen by said Society, for said purpose, shall act in concurrence with my executors in investing said sum, *provided*, that whenever, if ever, said Society shall fail to support the preaching of the gospel and a regularly settled minister of the Congregational denomination for any unreasonable length of time, and provide annually by tax or in some other way a sum not less than Five Hundred Dollars for the support of preaching and the other necessary expenses of public worship in said Society, then the said sum of Five Thousand Dollars shall revert to and be paid over to my children, or to their heirs by right of representation.

Fourteenth, I give and bequeath to the Baptist Religious Society in the west part of the town of Royalston, the sum of Twenty Five Hundred Dollars, to be kept and applied as a fund, the income of which shall be appropriated annually or semi-annually to the support of Gospel preaching, and public worship in said Society, and it is my will that a Committee, to be chosen by said Society for such purpose, shall act in concurrence with my Executors, in investing said sum, *provided*, that whenever said Society shall neglect to raise by subscription or otherwise a sum not less than One Hundred and Fifty Dollars per annum for the support of preaching, and public worship, the said sum of Twenty Five Hundred Dollars shall revert to and be paid over to my children or to their heirs by right of representation.

Fifteenth, I give and bequeath to the Second Congregational Society of Royalston, at South Royalston, so called, the sum of Twenty Five Hundred Dollars ($2500,) to be held as a fund, the income of which shall be appropriated annually or semi-annually to the support of Gospel preaching in said Society; and it is my will that a Committee, to be chosen by said Society, for such purpose, shall act in concurrence with my Executors in the investing of said sum, *provided*, that whenever, if ever, said Society shall fail to support preaching, or to maintain a regularly organized Society at South Royalston, or whenever, if ever, that part of Royalston now known as South Royalston, shall be set off from said town of Royalston, then, this sum of Twenty Five Hundred Dollars shall revert to and be paid over to my children or their heirs by right of representation.

Sixteenth, I give and bequeath to the town of Royalston the sum of Five Thousand Dollars ($5000,) to be held and applied as a fund, the income of which shall be appropriated and paid over for the benefit and use of Common Schools in said town, the said income to be divided among the several School Districts in like manner as the school money raised by the town shall be divided; and it is my will that a Committee, to be chosen by the town for such purpose, shall act in concurrence with my Executors in investing said sum, and that every year a Committee shall be chosen by the town at a legally called town meeting who shall have the charge and oversight of such investment and shall report annually to the town the condition and income of the same, *provided*, however, that whenever the said town of Royalston shall neglect to keep, or cause to be kept, in a good state of repair, the new cemetery now being established on the ground recently purchased of C. H. Maxham, that is to say, shall neglect to maintain in good order and condition the said ground, fence, gate, and receiving tomb therein, then this sum of Five Thousand Dollars shall revert to and be paid over to my children and their heirs by right of representation."

Mr. Bullock, who was for some years a trustee of Amherst College, was also the donor of the fine Telescope, that now crowns the College Observatory.

NOTE I.—PAGE 36.   WILD BEASTS AND GAME.

Story tellers often keep on hand a store of Indians, Bears, Wolves, or something of the kind, to *put in* for the entertainment of their auditors, especially the juveniles. Nor do grave historians scorn to relieve and enliven their pages, by working up materials of this kind, when honestly to be had. *We* are unfortunate about the Indians, having, after diligent search, found nothing more than a few probable stone arrow-heads, pestles &c., of their handi-work, and some, not so probable, traditions of Red-Skins, seen among the brakes and alders, along the margins of our ponds and streams. We give the Indians over.

Not so the Bears and Wolves. These made quite a figure in the early days.—Bears crossed the wood-mans path, and alarmed the berry pickers in the clearings. Mrs. Reuben Walker, whose first home, after her marriage, was on the place now occupied by Franklin H. Goddard—formerly the Asa Bacheller place—rehearsed to one of this committee, when he was a boy, her adventure with a white-faced bear. She was out for black berries; and seeing some fine ones, whose canes grew up by the side, and interlaced with the dead branches of a fallen hemlock, she worked her way to them along the trunk of the prostrate tree. While employed in gathering the tempting berries, she made a false step and fell among the bushes—landing almost *upon* a bear. Of course, she screamed, and ran. The bear ran too,—but in the opposite direction.

But the bears did worse than give the settlers an occasional fright. They feloniously made way with sheep and calves from the pastures, and sometimes broke into the folds, by night, and took their fill of choice mutton. Various modes were adopted for punishing these marauders. Traps were made of logs, and Bruin, like a great many other pleasure seekers, found it easier to get into these inviting accommodations, than to get safely out again. After awhile iron traps came into vogue; but these sometimes proved hog-traps, as well. Thus, a bear having broken into the fold of Nathan Reed, who lived on the John Holman place, now so called, and made a supper off of one of his sheep, he applied to his neighbor Bigsby to set his iron trap for the depredator the next night. Unfortunately, however, his neighbor Piper's hog stumbled into the trap during the evening, both to his own hurt, and the spoiling of the nice little after-scene, got up especially for the bear. There was so much noise and disturbance about the premises in consequence of this mis-adventure, that Mrs. Bruin declined coming for her supper in that locality; but went over to the fold of Mr. Bemis, where she made free with one of his sheep. Mr. Bigsby tried his trap, the next night, near this second scene of depredation; and sure enough, the bear walked into it, this time, losing both her supper and her life. When dressed she weighed about 300 lbs.

Bear hunts were frequently organized, and the common enemy was hunted down in this way. The last bear hunt, in Royalston, came off as recently as 1829. A bear was seen in the outskirts of Hardscrabble, a rude piece of woods, lying south of the "the city." The next day the people rallied in force, with guns and dogs, determined to take the bear dead or alive. He was uncovered early in the day; but gave a gratuitous entertainment to his pursuers, which lasted till near nightfall, when two well directed shots, by Cyrus Davis and James Buffum, brought him to the ground. The huntsmen gathered to the *finale*, and one of them, our now venerable townsman, Adriel White, more venturesome than prudent, got a *hug*, the marks of which he carries to this day.

Wolves were more numerous, and dangerous, than the Bears; though they sooner abandoned the town. The early settlers used to see them in the evening twilight, stealing abroad, and, in the hours of breaking day, returning to their coverts, generally without noise, and several of them together, following each other in single file. In the night, however, they held high carnival on the open meadows, and, during the winter, upon the ponds. Dea. Enos Metcalf, who lived on the high lands just west of Long Pond, used to describe their howling as *frightful*. Upon visiting their rendezvous, the next day, the grass or snow as the case might be, would be trodden as though a flock of sheep had been folded over night upon the spot. Woe to man or beast, abroad and unprotected in the night. The Wolves were almost sure to be upon their track, and hunt them down before morning. Our Bosworth story is far from incredible. His pine knot was a good arm of defence; and his strategy was admirable. But many a poor beast, that strayed from the pastures, and failed of being hunted up by its owners, paid the forfeit of its temerity with its life. The Wolves even made bold, when pressed with hunger, to adventure their attacks in the broad day. Benoni Peck, Esq., gives us an instance. His mother, her husband being absent one day, and she engaged in her domestic affairs within doors, heard their first and only cow bellowing, as though in affright or mortal pain. She shut up her four little ones, and went out to ascertain the cause of the unusual noise. Passing the hovel she armed herself with the pitch-fork, and hastened to the scene of disturbance, where she found the cow cornered among some logs, and a wolf rending her. Mrs. Peck rushed upon the ferocious creature, employing both lungs and fork with a will. The wolf beat a reluctant retreat; and the cow, though badly mangled, was saved by the heroism of her mistress.

Royalston, like most of the other towns, offered a *bounty* on wolves; and wolf-heads, came to hold a market value.

Wildcats, Catamounts, and Panthers, so called, were often heard in the woods, sometimes seen, and sometimes killed. We have several instances of the shooting, or taking of these dangerous animals; while all accounts agree, that the concerts they gave at night, around the cabins, camp-fires and coal-pits of the early settlers, put all that is ever executed of this kind, by their domestic cousins, deep into the shade.

Of course, game abounded in the forests, while the ponds and streams afforded good fishing grounds. Mr. Jones was not the only one to get sight of the moose; though we learn of none who made so romantic use of his trophies. Mrs. Nathan Cutting, whose *cosy* home, it will be remembered, was set back into the hill, east of where John Leathe now lives, once had the privacy of her domestic arrangements invaded by a large specimen of this family, which peered into her kitchen from the height above. Deer were more common, and many an antler graced the cabins of our fathers, while their larders could frequently boast the savory venison. Wild turkies were, for a long time, met with in flocks of 20, 50 or 100. There are those now living, who have seen them in the fall of the year, in large numbers, upon the meadows north of Long Pond. Asahel Davis shot a wild turkey gobbler, in 1808, that weighed 20 lbs.; and the Mrs. Walker, whose encounter with the bear has been told, is said to have run down a famous wild turkey upon the snow crust, with her dog. That our streams were once frequented by beavers, the remains of their dams still demonstrate, Fine specimens of the Otter have been, and still are, occasionally, taken in our waters. We have always had fox-hunters among us; and the baying of the hounds is still a common occurrence, in the season of fox-hunting

But the days of good hunting, trapping and fishing have gone by with us. Only the indomitable sportsman, who can hunt all day for a shot, or angle hours for a "nibble," have now any great enthusiasm in exploring our woods, or waters for game; while *wild beasts* are absolutely obsolete.

NOTE L.—PAGE 45. ROADS.

In 1753 the proprietors empowered a committee, consisting of Joseph Wilder, Caleb Dana, and John Chandler, to clear out a way, or ways, to their recent purchase, and lay their account before the Proprietors. Bills for this work were subsequently rendered and allowed; but no data remain for ascertaining the location of these thoroughfares. The settlers came in from almost every point of the compass, and the accounts we have of the difficulties which many parties encountered in making their way to their wilderness homes, indicate that no very commodious roads had been made. Within the township it was no better. To reach their settlements, to communicate with each other and the common center, each settler was left to his own resources. The roads were mere *trails* or paths marked by *blazed trees*, i. e. trees spotted with the ax. Present convenience, the necessity of the case, and the means at hand, determined where those paths should run, and how be constructed. The future was left to care for itself. Perhaps this was all that could have been expected of the settlers themselves in the first years of their advent. It might have been better had the Proprietors, consulting their own interests and the interests of their embryo town, taken this matter in hand at the beginning and opened ways to the settler's lots which they early laid out and designated, or had the town, incorporated so soon after its settlement began, been more thoughtful and provident of the future. As it was, however, these hap-hazard and circuitous *trails* of the first settlers became, for the most part, and by authority, the *roads* of the town. Now that the forests are felled and the country opened, it is easy to detect the errors of this system, or want of system, in road-making; but not so easy to remedy them. In vain do we regret the large elbows that should have been cut across, and the hills that might have been so easily avoided.

It is curious to study the records of road-making, road-changing &c., as they are plentifully scattered through our portly books. Down to 1797, 92 roads had been laid out by the selectmen, accepted by the town and ordered to be constructed. In addition to these several public-roads, at least one "*bridal*" road had been legalized; but whether the authorities sought, by this last named road, to bring forward the settlement of the town, or the clerk was at fault in his spelling, every one is at liberty to judge for himself.

During this period 15 roads had been discontinued, and six materially changed, or "turned". From $125, to $250, was the annual appropriation for road purposes, and 50 cts. allowed for a day's work upon the roads. In 1797 the appropriation was $466 67 the price of a days labor remaining the same.

In later times more of the old roads have been discontinued or changed; and new roads constructed upon later models. We have now about 80 miles of public highways and the annual appropriation is from ten to twelve hundred dollars,—sometimes raised as a money tax and expended by special committees, and sometimes it is *worked out* in the old-fashioned way. At present, however, the price of labor upon the roads is no longer determined by the town but follows the law of demand and supply, as in other cases. Road *mending* is not now the free and easy, not to say. *high* thing it used to be, filling the highways with men, boys, and oxen, all intent upon making a good thing of it, for themselves at least, several yoke of oxen hitched to the same plough, each yoke with a driver, two or more men riding upon the beam, and one burly fellow holding the handles, while the residue of the squad watch the process of ploughing, or leisurely pitch the furrow into the road; but now a single yoke of oxen, and two or three men with modern tools go forth to this business, and somehow it happens that more work is done and to better purpose by this corporal's guard, than used to be accomplished by the assembled wisdom and prowess of a whole neighborhood.

An extra appropriation is made for the repair of the larger bridges, and disbursed by the Selectmen as occasion requires.

In addition to these appropriations the town is liable to be called upon, often in a very considerable sum, for keeping the roads open in winter. The day of old-fashioned turnouts for snow-shovelling and snow treading is gone by; and the boys and steers are no longer called upon for volunteer services in the behalf of the public. It is suggested, with how much truth we do not undertake to say, that the old style disappeared with the taverns, that used to stand at almost every corner, and where, as also at the grand old stores, the road-breakers used to get a thorough warming after coming through the drifts. At all events this business is now done on a money basis, and as nobody can tell beforehand how much road-breaking will be required, no appropriation is made: but the town foots the bills in the Spring.

NOTE, M.—PAGE 45.   THE DOCTORS BACHELLERS.

In our early records we have the signatures of the heads of two families, by the name of Bacheller,—Dr. Stephen Bacheller, and Dea. John Bacheller; but they wrote their *sir* name differently. The Doct. wrote, Bachelder, and Dea., Bacheller. Doct. Stephen Bacheller, Jr. wrote his name after still another orthography, Batcheller.

In these Notes we have adopted the Deacon, as our authority, hoping in him, as the middle man to find the *golden means*.

We add here, an *abstract* of a "Biographical Notice" of the Doctors Bacheller, father and son, printed in "The Boston Medical and Surgical Journal." Vol. 39, No. 23.

Dr. Stephen Bacheller, Sen. was born at Grafton, Mass., and commenced the practice of his profession in Royalston, in the early settlement of the town, in fact when it was almost an entire wilderness. He was the first physician of the town, and there he continued to practice till his decease. He suffered much from the want of roads, and the condition of such as existed. He was obliged to travel by marked trees, in this and the neighboring towns, often by night, and frequently followed by bears and wolves; and to ford streams at the peril of his life. Add to this the roughness of the country in the north-western section of Worcester county, and some idea may be formed of the perils and dangers he had to endure in the discharge of his professional duties. Yet he never refused to respond to the calls of his lot, whatever the raging of the storm, the darkness of the night, the dangers of the way, or the poverty of the patients. His ride was very extensive. He was remarkable for his kindness and attention to the poor, never compelling payment from them for medical services. Early in life he made a profession of religion by joining the Congregational Church in Royalston.

His son, Dr. Stephen Bacheller, Jr. received his preparatory education at the Academies of Chesterfield, N. H., and New Salem, of this State. He devoted much attention to the study of the Latin Language, and had a good knowledge of Greek. He commenced the study of medicine with his father, but spent the latter period of his pupilage under the instruction of the late Dr. Henry Wells, of Montague, one of the most distinguished physicians of New England.

At the age of 22, he began the practice of his profession in Truro, on the Cape. This was in the autumn or winter of 1800. He remained at Truro three years; when, at the solicitation of his father, who began to feel some of the infirmities of age, he returned to his native town, and commenced business with him in 1803. And it is a fact worthy of notice, that the father and son practiced in town during the long period of 80 years,—the father 35 years before the son commenced with him, and the son 45 years from his return to Royalston in 1803.

As a physician, the latter certainly held a high and very respectable rank and was greatly esteemed by his professional brethren. He probably had, for many years, a more extensive consultation business than any other physician in the County, and perhaps in the State. He was highly honored by the Mass. Medical Society, of which he became a fellow June 1, 1824, and continued his connection to the time of his decease. He was one of the most punctual attendants at its annual meetings, often riding from Royalston to Boston,—70 miles or more,—in his gig the day before the meeting, and returning home, in the same manner, the day after. He was for many years one of the Counsellors of the Society; two years its Vice President; and one of the delegates from this Society, in May, 1848, to the

American Medical Association, whose session that year was held in Baltimore. He was one of the founders of the District Society, for Worcester Co., and for some years its President.

The number of medical students, who spent a part or the whole of their pupilage with him, was about 40, many of whom have proved respectable and even eminent physicians. He was ambitious to keep pace with the improvements in the profession, procuring and reading the latest and most approved periodical publications, and standard works. He was an early riser, and devoted his whole time to his library and his patients. His professional charges were unusually low; and like very many of his brethren he was negligent in collecting his debts, especially if the debtor was poor. The widow and the orphan were constantly applying to him for advice and counsel; and he often assisted them to his own pecuniary detriment.

Independently of his professional worth he was highly esteemed by his townsmen as a valuable citizen, representing his native town in the State Legislature, holding the office of a Justice of the Peace, and serving in various municipal offices. He gave all his influence in favor of the cause of Temperance, and contributed liberally for the support of the institutions of religion, education &c. He literally died in the harness, having practiced in two of the adjoining towns on the day of his death, and on his return, deposited his vote for Presidential Electors at the town-house. He died at the house of a near neighbor, where he called apparently well; but soon complained of feeling faint,—leaned back in his chair, and called for a glass of water, but before it could be handed him, he was dead.

NOTES N, O, P, & Q.—PAGES 49: 50: 52: 53.   REVOLUTIONARY PERIOD.

During this Period the people of Royalston, in common with those of other towns, were often called upon to canvass, in their legal capacity, the grave questions of State then in aggitation; and to share the common burdens of those eventful years. The rapid sketch, given by Mr. Bullock, brings out the salient points and produces an impression as grateful as it is just. The action of the town was not only in harmony with the general spirit of those grand old times, but manifestly the result of mature deliberation and sound and comprehensive theories. Indeed it is marvellous, that a community, so distant from the centres of population and business, so lately brought together, and so occupied and even pressed with the cares of a new settlement, should be able to address themselves with dignity and effect to the work of a great political revolution. But even here, and under such circumstances, there was the intelligence and statesmanship, even, which insured the apprehension of duty, and brought out the resources of the people in their full strength.

The fuller history of this period, so unconsciously imprinted on the records of the times, justifies and deepens the impression above referred to; while, as the order and significance of its details are gathered and apprehended, the problem of popular government grows luminous. If, in such circumstances, it is practicable to find committees of correspondence, and of safety, worthy to be consulted in the debates and decisions of a national crisis, and delegates competent to take in hand the radical reconstruction of the state, then, surely, free institutions are in order, the people may be trusted, and it is their prerogative to rule. Certainly the experiment in Royalston, and as tested by the fruits of a hundred years, shows that our fathers were ripe for freedom, and competent, alike in Church and State, wisely to assert and maintain popular constitutional liberty.

As early as 1773, while yet the hour of the Revolution had not struck, the citizens of Royalston put themselves in corres. pondence with the central committee in Boston, and through them with the other towns of the Province, that "the sentiments" of the people might have utterance in the ear of government, and that unity of counsel might prevail in meeting the encroachments of the Crown and Parliament. To this they added a committee of Safety, like the former, affiliated with others through the Province, and continued by annual elections till the final triumph of the American cause. Prominent and familiar names fill the lists of these potent agencies in the interests of Justice and Liberty.

It was before Royalston had begun to send Representatives to the General Court, that the final breach between it and the Provincial governor occured. Gov. Gage, by his proclamation of Sept. 1, 1774, had convoked said court to meet at Salem on the 5th of October following. On the last Wednesday of the previous May, the government for the year had been duly organized; and the councillors, then chosen and qualified, held their office. according to the charter, during the year. Meanwhile Parliament had passed the "Regulating Act," in which, among other things, aimed at the subversion of our ancient Charter, the appointment of councillors was taken from the Assembly and vested in the crown. The King, eager to begin the work of humbling Massachusetts, sent to Gage a new list of Councillors, at the same time with the Regulation Act. Both came to hand Aug. 6, 1774; and the new Councillors were forthwith summoned to their post by a writ of Mandamus; hence their title *Mandamus Councillors*. The Province, therefore, had two set of councillors, one holding office under the charter, another holding their positions by virtue of the King's Mandamus. In these circumstances Gage had issued his proclamation convoking the General Court. But he was soon made aware that the old councillors intended to take their seats as usual; and further that the Mandamus Councillors could not be present to contest those seats without a stronger escort than he could then afford them. Nay, no sooner had the people become aware of this move, and that there were men among themselves, who had consented to take office in the subversion of the charter, then they gave these gentlemen such indications of their sentiments, that, of the six and thirty who had received the writ, more than twenty revoked their acceptance, or declined to attend at Salem, while the rest fled to the British army at Boston for personal safety; and they fled none too soon: for there was not a town in the whole province where a Mandamus councillor, whatever had been his previous standing, was safe, till he had thrown up his commission and publicly foresworn all future complicity with the royal government in its attempts to overthrow the ancient liberties. Isaac Royal was one of those councillors who preferred to fly to Boston, and ultimately to fly the country, rather than give up the royal commission he had received from the king.

Gage now found himself in a dilemma. He had lately come from the king, assuring him, that, with four regiments, he would play the "lion," with his refractory subjects across the waters. But he was check-mated on the first move. He sought to escape by a second proclamation, issued Sept. 28, in which, without either proroguing or dissolving the General Court, he informed the members elect, that he should not meet them at Salem on the 5th of October, and discharged them from giving their attendance.

Ninety of the members met, notwithstanding, and after waiting two days for the Governor, proceeded to business. They first sat in judgment upon the second proclamation; pronounced it unconstitutional and void, and having resolved themselves into a Provincial Congress, and adjourned to meet at Concord on the eleventh, with such other delegates as might see cause to join them. On the eleventh they met 260 strong, put John Hancock at their head as President, and on the fourteenth sent a message to the Governor, informing him, that, for want of an Assembly, they had convened in a Provincial Congress.

This was inaugurating a new order of things, and it behooved the people to pass upon it. Royalston elected to go with the patriotic delegates, and against the usurpations of the governor; and we find the name of *Henry Bond* upon the roll of this Congress. A second convened at Cambridge, Feb. 1, 1775; held an adjourned session at Concord and another at Watertown, and was disssolved May 29th of the same year. Upon this *Nahum Green* attended, participating also in those early and momorable passages at arms, during those months, which transferred our controversy from the forum to the battle-fields of a seven years' war.

On this new theatre Royalston kept herself continually represented, not by solitary delegates, but full quotas, whose names. as far as we have been able to gather them, are given below.

Our archives have no list; but from the votes of the town, from bills, orders and receipts, scattered through the town records of this period, from the records of deaths occurring in camp, or on the war-paths,—from the pension lists, and from the sacred memories of descendants, relatives, and friends, we have constructed this roll of our

REVOLUTIONARY SOLDIERS.

NAHUM GREEN.

Col. Ebenezer Newel,
Maj. John Norton,
Capt. Jonathan Sibley,
Capt. Enoch Whitmore,
Lt. Edward Holman,
Lt. Nathan Wheeler,
David Copeland.
Ammi Falkner,
John Davis. Jr.,
Squier Davis,
Sylvester Davis.
John Ellis,
Nathan Bliss,
Eliphalet Richardson,
Abijah Richardson.
David Bullock.

Lt. Jonas Allen,
Lt. James Work,
Lt. Micah French,
Silas Cutting,
Bezaleal Barton.
Samuel Barton.
Moses Walker,
Joel Stockwell,
Ebenezer Burbank,
Benjamin Clark,
——— Perham.
Josiah Waite,
Nathan B. Newton,
Joseph Emerson,
Samuel W. Bowker,
Samuel Lewis,

Jonathan Wellington,
Rogers Chase,
Benjamin Leathe,
Isaac Nichols,
William Clement, 2d,

Nathaniel Jacobs,
Benajah Woodbury,
David Cook,
William Clement,
Jonathan Gale,

Timothy Armstrong.

It is probable that some of the above names, which we derived from the pension lists, belonged to persons who were not citizens of Royalston before the Revolution, but settled here immediately after leaving the war. As we found it impossible to discriminate such cases with certainty, we have given all the early settlers, who drew pensions.

In addition to the above, there was a large company of the men of Royalston, who shouldered their muskets, upon short notice, and marched to repel the invasion of the "Northern Army," in 1777. But General Gates had put a period to that enterprise, before the rallying forces from this section could join him, having defeated Burgoyne in the battle of Stillwater, Sept. 17th, and again, more thoroughly, in the battle of Saratoga, Oct. 7th, and compelled him to capitulate his entire force, Oct. 17. These volunteers were ordered back to their homes.

Our experience in the late war with the Rebellion enables us to appreciate, somewhat more fully, the business and the importance of the business, which, to so large an extent, engaged the attention of the towns in their legal meetings, during this Revolutionary period. But even this experience does not suggest all the sublime features of the original struggle. We had only to see to it, that constitutions, laws and liberties, already established, and long enjoyed, were neither crushed out, nor *infracted;* but our fathers had, first of all, to break from off them the yoke of a mighty foreign power, and then,—nay, in the very height of this great effort, and amid all the exigencies of blazing war, to originate, and foster into strength and maturity, a new form of civil life; and all this, of course, when there were no constituted civil authorities to undertake the work for them. It must be brought before the primary assemblies of the people at every step, and in all its stages, while every town was straining all its powers to furnish men and means to ensure that triumph in the conflict of arms, without which constitutions and laws would be useless.

As early as 1776, Massachusetts moved in the direction of a State Constitution. It was put to the several towns whether the General Court of 1777 should be chosen with the understanding that one part of their duty should be to form a Constitution. Royalston went heartily for the measure. The resulting constitution was read in the April meeting of 1778; but action thereon was postponed till the May meeting; when the town "voted not to approve of said Constitution as it now stands. Voted to approve of said Constitution in part," and a committee of seven men was chosen to make such alterations in, and remarks upon, the work of the General Court, both the parts disapproved and those that were approved, as they might deem needful in order to convey to the Court the sense of the people. The committee reported at an adjourned meeting,—the last Wednesday in May, when the town "heard the form of government composed by the committee, read over and again, and voted unanimously to approve of the same. Number voted, 76." The clerk was directed to make out an attested copy of this document, and transmit it to the Secretary's Office, "as truly expressive of the sense of this town respecting government which they are desirous may be established as soon as possible."

This effort failing, it was submitted to the people whether the next General Court should call a convention for the sole purpose of framing a constitution. Royalston again answered in the affirmative, and responded to the subsequent precept of the General Court, by choosing Silvanus Hemenway " to join in convention at Cambridge on the first day of September next (1779) to form a constitution of Government for the State of Massachusetts Bay."

The "Frame of Government proposed by the Convention was laid before the town May 25th, 1780; and laid over to be acted upon at an adjourned meeting on the 31st. A town meeting was held on that day under a distinct warrant, and its doings thereon duly recorded; but no record is to be found of the adjourned meeting. The doughty Captain of "Louisburg and Crown Point memory," seems, for once at least, to have forgotten himself. It may seem the less strange if we state, that John Fry was moderator of each of these meetings,—clerk of the Town, a delegate elect—in the place of Mr. Hemenway—to the second session of the State Convention, and Representative elect to the General Court. With so many duties and honors to look after, shall we not plead a mitigation of censure, though he has left us no record of the final action of the town in regard to our excellent State Constitution.

A Convention had held one session at Concord, and adjourned to meet again Oct. 1, 1779. The town was warned and came together to act upon the following article, which indicates the objects at the Convention aforesaid. "To hear the proceedings of the Convention at Concord on account of settling prices of commodities bought and sold [within the State] and act on said affair as the town may think proper."

It seems that the currency had become so deranged as seriously to affect trade and business. In the absence of legal remedies, the effort was made, sometimes by the concurrence of several towns, sometimes by County, and sometimes by State Conventions, to regulate by mutual agreement and recommendation, the prices at which commodities should be bought and sold, and labor performed. It was but a temporary expedient while yet the nation was struggling for her life; and therefore without any pretence of law, or legal authority. But it was hoped that it might have *moral* force, and it stands as an illustration of the brave and considerate patriotism of the times. A godly old patriot in New Hampshire, interested in encouraging similar movements, when told they would be of no use, for people in the absence of law, would sell and buy as they could, is said to have replied,—'Any man who will not hear the voice of our Convention, would not hear, though one should arise from the dead.'

The town acted upon the article above stated, Aug. 16, 1779, and chose Henry Bond to attend the next session of the Convention, which was to meet the first Wednesday of October.

In due time the result of said Convention came before the town, when a Committee, consisting of Capt. Fry, Wm. Town, Lieut. Chase, Henry Bond, Lieut. Wheeler, Dea. Woodbury, and Peletiah Metcalf, was chosen "to set prices on the sundry commodities bought and sold in town, agreeable to the instructions of the Convention at Concord."

We have not been able to find the *schedule* of prices adopted, or to ascertain the effect of the measure upon the people, or business of the town.

There is one record relating to the Continental Congress, which, for its brevity and point, deserves to be recited. The town had been called together to act upon the following articles.

"2. To hear the Resolves of Congress."

3. To act thereon as the town may think proper. The town met Jan. 28th, 1778, and their doings are thus set down.

" 2. Read the Resolves of Congress.

3. Voted to accept and abide by them."

We close this note with a single extract, illustrating the action of the town in the matters referred to on the 53rd page.

" Jan. 8, 1781. The Committee, appointed by the town to make an average of the cost of the present war, met and appointed Mr. Wm. Town, Clerk of the Committee.

First question: How long back shall the property be taxed in the proposed average? Ans. All charges that have arisen in the year 1780.

2. Is it the opinion of the Committee that those persons that have done service in other towns be allowed for their services by this town, as a debt of this town? Ans. No.

3. Is it the opinion of the Committee that every class of men, for the same service at the same time and distance, shall be allowed equally? Ans. Yes.

4. How many times "old way" shall the cost of the war be doubled in "New Emission," to make it equal to the old way? Ans. Forty-five shillings in New Emission.

5. How far back shall those persons be taxed for the charge of the war, that have moved into town since the commencement of the war? Ans. The expenses since they came to town.

6. What shall be done with those persons that have done more than their proportion in the war before they come into town? Ans. It shall be left discretionary with the assessors in conjunction with the selectmen.

7. Shall any persons, whose credit is higher than their present tax, draw any of said credit out of the Treasury of this town until the close of the war? Ans. No.

The above articles were approved by the town.

JOHN BACHELLER, Moderator."

NOTE R.—PAGE 56. THE LAST WAR WITH GREAT BRITIAN.

The majority in Royalston laid no claim to special enthusiasm in this war. The national policy, which at length brought it on, had not been at all approved, and early, earnest and harmonious town action, similar to that in other towns, was had, to prevent if possible, the out-break. The Town heard, and voted a Petition to the President of the United States, in 1808, 'praying him that the embargo, in whole or in part, may be suspended, according to the powers vested in him by Congress.' The next year, they chose a committee, consisting of Joseph Esterbrook, Stephen Bacheller Jr., John Norton, Isaac Metcalf, and Rufus Bullock, to draft a Petition to the General Court to take measures to redress the greviances arising from the policy of the National Government. The committee reported a petition which was adopted by the town; and, as giving us some idea of the men, and the *spirit* of the times, we deem it relevant to the object we have in hand, to give a few paragraphs of the document.

"The inhabitants of the Town of Royalston, legally assembled in Town Meeting for the purpose of taking into consideration the present unprecedented and very alarming situation of our public affairs, hereby represent, that when there is a dereliction from the first principles, when there is a practical departure from what is warranted by the constitution, in those that lead in government, then there is a call to vigilance and exertion to prevent the progress of the evil. Notwithstanding it has been recently intimated from high authority that the people in town meeting &c., are not capable of judging of the propriety or impropriety of the measures of government, and that there are stages when an end must be put to debate, yet, so long as we consider our National and State Constitutions the supreme law of our land, we shall, agreably to the rights therein secured to us, (which rights we are determined never to relinquish,) take the liberty, on all important and portentous (issues,) particularly when those rights are invaded and trampled upon, to assemble in orderly and peaceable manner to make our grievances known, and to use all proper and constitutional means to have them redressed.

We have seen with anxiety a system of measures pursued which has paralized industry and enterprise, discouraged our farmers, and embarrassed our merchants, brought distress upon all classes of our citizens, and produced the greatest temptation for an illicit trade perhaps ever known.

We are firmly attached to our National and State constitutions, and cheerfully pledge our lives and everything we hold dear to support them. We are also firmly attached to a Union of the States and should view with horror and detestation any attempts to sever them, or to discountenance that friendship and harmony that ought to subsist between them."

The above will suffice for our object, in the introduction of this document.

In 1812 the town was called together again, "to see what measures to adopt relative to the distressing situation of our country, and act in concert with millions of American citizens to take all peaceable and Constitutional means, if possible to avert the horrors of war." Again the town chose a Committee to draft resolutions, heard and adopted them, and chose a delegation to attend a Convention at Worcester, then about to convene, to take into consideration the same absorbing subject.

But the war came; and Royalston met her responsibilities under the same, if not with the enthusiasm of partisans, yet with the steadiness of loyal citizens. When men were detached to serve in the Federal armies appropriations were made for them.

During the severe campaign of 1814, while the veteran troops of England were fighting desperately along the frontier of Niagara, and getting desperately punished at Chippewa, and Lundy's Lane, their naval force were threatening our Northern Sea-coast. They had already run up to Essex, on the Connecticut, and destroyed the shipping there to a large amount. Troops were therefore concentrated upon the sea-board for coast defense. It was in the prosecution of this object that the *Grenadiers*, a newly formed independent organization in Royalston, were called to Boston. They got their orders Saturday night, Aug. 9th, 1814; and were to march at once. They mustered the next day, attended divine service with their friends, and started for the capital of the State.

They were discharged after 35 days service and returned home without casuality.

This company, whose Roll, as it stood in 1814, we give below, kept up its organization down to a late period, and always sustained a high reputation. It will be observed that several of its original members rose to the command of the old 5th Regt.. to which it was attached, also that one of the privates, William Chase, Jr., afterwards commanded the company. There was a long line of Captains, from citizens subsequently joining the company.

We designate those of this company, since deceased, by the star.

Capt. Benj. Brown, Pro'd Col. 5th Regt., 2d Brig., 7th Div.
Lieut. Benoni Peck, " Capt. Grenadiers.
Ensign* W. Newton, Pro'd Col. 5th Regt., 2d Brig., 7th Div.
Sergeant Isaac Gale, 2d.
  " Elmer Newton, Pro'd Col. 5th Regt., 2d Brig., 7th Div.
  " Alanson White.
  " *Jonah Walker.
Corporal, Thomas Norton,
  " *Josiah Wheeler, Pro'd Col. 5th Regt., 2d Brig., 7th Div.
  " *Moses Tyler,
  " David Thurston.

MUSICIANS.

*Joseph Peirce, *Silas Peirce, Edson Clark, Silas Metcalf, James Peirce.

PRIVATES.

Luke Bemis, *Nathan Bemis, Jonas Brewer Jr., William Chase Jr., John Chamberlain Jr., *John Dexter, *Elias Emerson, *John Eaton, *Chauncy Forbush, *Moses Garfield, John Hill, Hiram

Lewis, *Benj. Leathe, Jr., Russel Morse, Chauncy Peck, *John Prescott, Chandler Peabody, *Thomas Rogers, *Stephen Richardson, *Reuben Stockwell, Isaac Stockwell, *Simeon Stockwell, *Joseph Stockwell, Jonathan Stockwell, Tarrant Stockwell, *John B. Walker, *Asa Walker, Nathaniel Wilson, Jr.

NOTE, S.—PAGE 58.   SOLDIERS IN THE WAR WITH THE REBELLION.

We give below, in response to the noble words of the centennial orator, the names of those men, who volunteered and served on the successive quotas of Royalston during the late war. Some of them have now returned to the pursuits of peaceful industry among us; some have gone into business elsewhere, and some,—alas! such, and so many, as we could have yielded only in such a cause, will come back no more. Yet they live in the memory of that sublimely patriotic devotion which had classic utterance in the words of Warren, when he broke from his deprecating friends to participate, as a private, in the battle of Bunker Hill,—"*It is pleasant and becoming to die for one's country.*"

Most of our soldiers served in the 21st, 25th, 36th, and 53rd Regts. The last named Regt., was for nine months. We are indebted to Adjutant General Wm. Schouler for material aid in perfecting this Roll.

The 21st Regiment left for the seat of war, Aug. 23, 1861, and was mustered out Aug. 30, 1864. The names, on its muster in, or out Roll, and serving on our quota are as follows:—

	Mustered in	
Nathan S. Day,	Aug. 23, '61	Dis'd for disability July 9, 1863.
C. A. Clark,	July 19,	·· Date of muster-out, or discharge lost.
Benj. F. Flagg,	Aug. 23,	·· Re-enlisted July 1, '64, Transfered to 57th Regt.
Joseph Gamer,	July 19,	·· Date of muster out or discharge lost.
Jonas Greeley,	Aug. 23,	·· Discharged for disability, Apr. 10, '63, Re-enlisted in 57th Regt.
Henry E. Knight,	·· ··	·· Re-enlisted Jan. 1, '64, killed in battle of Wilderness, May 6, '64.
Chauncy Norcross,	Aug. 23,	·· Died of wounds incured at Roanoke Island, N. C. Feb. 21, '62.
Sidney S. Heywood,		Served on detached duty.
Franklin A. Eddy,	July 19, '61	Dis'd for disability, Apr. 20 '62.

Besides these we have the following names, as serving in this Regt., but whose names do not appear on the Rolls of the Adjutant's office, John Barrus, Marshall Barrus, Addison S. Bradish, Nelson Rice, Charles Pope, Patrick Manning, (dead) Edwin Vose, (dead) Wm. H. Sprague, (dead) and Henry H. Higgins.

The 25th Regt. left for the seat of War Oct. 31, '61. A part of the men were mustered out at the expiration of their three years' service, but the Regt. was not till July 25, '65.

	Mustered in	
George W. Barrett,	Oct. 8, '61.	Re-enlisted Jan. 2. '64, Captured at Drury's Bluff, Va., May 16, '64, died at Andersonville, Ga.
Joel S. Bosworth,	·· ··	·· Captured at Drury's Bluff, Va., May 16, '64, died, at Andersonville, Ga,
George Brown,	·· ··	·· Died of wounds received at White Hill, N. C. Dec. 16, 62.
Martin Burgess,	·· ··	·· Dis'd Oct. 8, 64, Expiration of term, wounded Jan, 3, '64.
Hosea A. Bosworth,	·· ··	·· Dis'd of wounds received at Coal Harbor, Va. June 3, '64, died on way home, July 10, '64.
Wm. H. Chase,	·· ··	·· Mustered out Oct. 20, 1864.
John S. Chase,	·· 17,	·· Capt'd at Cold Harbor, June 3, 1864, died at Andersonville Ga.
Arthur E. Clement,	·· 8,	·· Mustered out Oct. 20, 1864.
Jay Davis,	·· 17,	·· ·· ·· ··
Byron Doane,	·· 8,	·· Re-enlisted Jan. 2, '64, Mustered out, July 25, '65.

	Mustered in	
David W. Day,	Oct. 17, '61	Discharged for disability June 3, '63.
Aaron A. Grant,	·· 8, ··	·· ·· ·· March 16, '62.
Wm. H. Howard,	Sept. 26, '61	Dis'd for disability Feb. 3, '62, Re-enlisted in 36th.
Stephen W. Martin,	·· ··	Died of fever at Newbern, N. C. May 16, 1862
Wesley D. Goddard,	·· ··	Dis'd for disability, Aug. 4, '62, Re-enlisted in 36, and killed in battle.
J. B. Meller.	·· ··	Mustered out Oct. 20, 1864.
Harlan P. Metcalf,	·· ··	On detached service, Mustered out.
Joseph T. Nichols,	·· ··	Dis'd for promotion June 10, 1863, com'd 2d, Lieut. in 55, July 10,' 63.
Nelson F. Peck,	·· ··	Corporal from Aug. 1, '64. Mustered out Oct. 20, 1864.
H. K. Sampson,	·· ··	Corporal from Apr. 27, '63. Re-enlisted Jan. 2, '64, Mustered out.
Alex'r. Stewart,	·· ··	Mustered out, Oct. 20, 1864.
James B. Smith,	·· ··	Com'd 1st, Lieut., Oct. 12, '61, Dis'd July 10, '62. Com'd Capt. in 36th Regt. Aug. 22, '62, and Maj. Oct. 12, 64.
Henry S. Wood,	·· ··	Dis'd Nov. 6, '63, by order of Secretary of War.
Lyman Wheeler,	·· ··	Sergeant to July 29, '63, Re-enlisted, wounded at Drury's Bluff, Va. May 16, '64.
George N. Wheeler,	Oct. 8, '61	Dis'd for disability, Aug. 4, '62.
Warren L. Wheeler,	·· ··	Corporal from June 24, '63, Mustered out Oct. 20, '64.

The 36th, left for the seat of War, Sept. 2, 1862, and was mustered out June, 8, 1865.

	Mustered in	
Adolphus Bussemius,	Aug. 27, '62	Dis'd for disability, March, 17, '65. wounded at Coal Harbor.
Wm. J. Barrus,	·· ··	Wounded June 3, '64. At Dale Hospital, Worcester.
Harrison C. Blake,	·· ··	Mustered out, June 8, 1865.
George W. Bowker,	·· ··	Paroled Prisoner, Annapolis, Md.
George L. Chase,	·· ··	Died of wounds at Campbell's Hospital, June, '64.
Wm. C. Doane,	·· ··	Dis'd Dec. 22, '62.
Benj. A. Fry,	·· ··	Mustered out, June 8, 1865.

	Mustered in	
Lucius F. French,	Aug. 27, '62	Mustered out June 8, 1865.
Sandford Giles,	" " "	Died of wounds rec'd at Spotsylvania. May 12 '64.
Wm. H. Howard,	" " "	Date of muster out or discharge not to be found.
Salem T. Hill.		Mustered out.
Charles S. Knight,	Feb. 18, '64	Transferred to 56th, by Secretary's order, June 6, '65.
Frank A. Osborn,	" 27, 62	Transferred to 56th by Secretary's order, June 6, '65.
Clarence E. King,	Aug. 27, '62	Died of fever at Nicholsville, Ky., Aug. 23, '63.
Henry Russell,	" " "	Died of wounds near Petersburg, Va. Aug. 10, '64.
George W. Raymond,	Jan. 13, '64	Died of wounds at Coal Harbor, Va. Jan. 4, 64.
John Shepardson,	Aug. 27, '62	Killed in action. June 17, '64.
Nathan S. Tandy,	" " "	Dis'd for disability, Feb. 26, '63.
Otis K. Upham,	" " "	Mustered out.
Arthur Peirce,	" " "	Died of Cholera Morbus, at Hartwood, Va. Nov. 19, '62.
Benj. Potter,	" " "	Dis'd for disability, Sept. 21, '63.
Asaph M. White,	" " "	Corporal from Apr 1, '65. Must'd out.
Rollin N. White,	" " "	Died of wounds, at Harwood Hospital June 25, '64.
Stephen P. White,	" " "	Died of fever, Annapolis, Md. May 5, '64.
Joseph Walker,	" " "	Dis'd for disability, Oct. 29, '63.

The 53d Regt., (nine months) left for the war, Nov. 29, 1862, and were mustered out Sept. 2, 1863.

	Mustered in	
Benj. H. Brown,	Oct. 17, '62	1st Lieut. Mustered out Sept. 2, '63.
Emerson E. Bissell,	" " "	Corporal, " " " " "
Willis H. Barton,	" " "	Re-enlisted in 57th (2d veteran) Mustered out July 30, '65
Amos B. Bosworth,	" " "	Mustered out, Sept. 2, '63.
Joseph W. Bosworth,	" " "	Dis'd at Baton Rouge, La.—Died soon after getting home of chronic diarrhea.
Edward W. Cross,	" " "	Mustered out, Sept. 2, '63.
Uri C. Day,	" " "	Died of Chronic Diarrhea, at Baton Rouge, La.

	Mustered in	
Bernard Doane,	Oct. 17, '62	Dis'd at New York, Jan. 8, '63.
Martin Fallan,	.. ..	..Mustered out, Sept. 2, '63.
Alonzo French,	.. ..	..Corporal from May 1st, '63. Mustered out, Sept. 2 '63.
James N. Hunt,	.. ..	..Mustered out, Sept. 2, '63.
George L. Hancock,	.. ..	..Died at Carrolton, La., March 8, 63, of Chronic Diarrhea.
George W. Knight,	.. ..	..Corporal. Died at New Orleans, Apr. 10, '63.
John S. Moore,	.. ..	..Mustered out, Sept. 2, 1863.
Henry C. Moore,	.. ..	..Died of Chronic Diarrhea at New Orleans, Apr. 29, '63.
Andrew J. Norcross,	.. ..	..Mustered out, Sept. 2, '63.
Herman M. Patridge,	.. ..	..Pro'd Q. M. Sargeant, Oct. 17, 1862. Mustered out, Sept. 2, '63.
Asa A. Palmer,	.. ..	..Mustered out, Sept. 2, '63.
George W. Russell,	.. ..	.. " " " " "
Geo. O. Richardson,	.. ..	.. " " " " "
W. W. Sherwin,	.. ..	.. " " " " "
Warren Thatcher,	.. ..	.. " " " " "
Charles E.. Tenney,		Died at New Orleans, La. Apr. 26, '63, of Chronic Diarrhea.
John M. Wood,	.. :	..Died at Baton Rouge, La. May 15, '63. of chronic diarrhea.
George W. Wood,	.. ..	..Dis'd for disability, Jan. 1, '63.
Adriel C White,	.. ..	..Corporal from Oct. 17, 62, Mustered out Sept. 2, '63.

The 32d Regt. were organized for garrison duty at Fort Warren. It was sent to the seat of war in time to be engaged in the battles before Richmond, at Antietam, and Fredericksburg; and we have the following men of this Regt,—a three years' Regt.

	Mustered in	
Allen F. Fish,	Nov. 28, '61	Dis'd at Convalescent Camp, Va. in Jan. 1863
Ambrose Clark,	.. 25, ..	Dis'd for disability, March 2, 1862.
James Townsend,	.. .. ..	Died of disease at Harrison Landing, Va., Aug. 2, 1862.
Elkanah Paine,	.. .. ..	Re-enlisted Jan. 1st, Sergeant, Mustered out June 7, 1865.

Wm. Welsh served in the 15th Regt.,—dead.

Henry L. Bennett in the 6th Battery.

George A. Flagg in the 27th, Mustered in Dec. 14, '64. Dis'd for disability.

Prescott Metcalf, and Levi Bosworth, served as veterans in 27th.

Mirick Burgess and Aaron Rice enlisted in the N. H. 6th. John Nash, Danvas Miles, and George Miles, served in the N. H. 2d. The latter was killed in action.

We learn from the Adjutant General's Office, that 27 of our men were mustered out June 26, 1865; and gathered from the Adj't. General's Report of 1863, and '64, that at the close of '63, the whole number of men called for from Royalston was 92, and that the town had then furnished 106; and that at the close of 1864 we still had a surplus of 5 men.

Franklin Brown was the only drafted man of Royalston, who responded in person to the draft.

Phineas S. Newton put in a substitute—a colored man—paying $500.

The following persons paid the $300, commutation. Joseph Shepardson, John B. Walker, Andrew J. Bliss, Phillip H. Bliss, A. Dwight Raymond, George E. Peirce, George S. Raymond, Reuben Pratt, Wilson Carroll, Charles A. King, Silas Wyman Jr., Lysander Howard, Brazia French, John W. Leathe, ——— Gun, Caleb Stockwell, Chilson Bosworth Jr., Abijah Whitmore.

It may not be out of place to insert here the names of persons born, or bred in Royalston, who we happen to know have served in this war, though not on our quotas. Of course our personal knowledge cannot be supposed to have gathered all who would properly belong to this list. We give such as we are able, without special investigation.

Major General Lysander Cutler, of Wisconsin.

Lieut. Colonel Charles Cummings, of Vermont.

Capt. Andrew J. Richardson. of Wisconsin.
" Henry J. Howe, of Pennsylvania..
Lieut. Silas Heywood, of New Hampshire.
Quarter Master Wm. O. Brown, of Fitchburg, Mass.
" " Edward A. Brown, now residing in Royalston.
Sergeant Major Harlan P. Patridge, of Fitchburg, Mass.

Jefferson Richardson, of N. H. (dead) George Fry, of N. H. (dead) John D. Emerson, of Athol, Mass. George H. Piper of Winchendon, Mass. James S. Piper, of Gardner, Mass. Lysander B. Piper, of Ill. Wellington White, of Michigan, Theodore Jones Hill, of Winchendon, Mass. Nelson Wood, of Athol, Mass. (dead) Quincy A. Shepardson, of Petersham, Mass. (dead)

NOTE T.—PAGE 58. EDUCATION.

Massachusetts, whether as a Province or a State, has always been true to the cause of Education. In the sale and settlement of her public lands they imposed conditions, looking to the establishment and nurture of common schools. In the sale of our territory, the General Court reserved one sixty third part of the whole purchase for this purpose, putting the purchasers under bonds to carry out their intention. The purchase was for 28.357 acres, exclusive of sundry private Grants already located within the territory. These were found to amount to 2.300 acres; making our territory, according to the public surveys, to consist of 30.657 acres. We have seen, (page 89.) that the purchasers, before they drew lots for themselves, set apart 520 acres for school land; which, instead of being only sixty-third part of their purchase, is one sixty-third part of 32.760 acres. They were not only just, but generous. It will be remembered, too, that Hon. Isaac Royal, by his will, gave the town 200 acres more for school purposes. Hence it appears that, through the provident forethought of the Government and the generosity of our Proprietors, 720 acres of our township were, from the first, sacredly appropriated to the cause of popular education.

This, indeed, was a good start in the right direction; and we have been more fortunate than some of our sister towns, in being able to give a good account of the school-land. The "Old School Fund," accruing from its sale, now amounts to $1500, and is invested, $1.000, in Notes and Mortgages on Real Estate, and $500, in U. S. Bonds. The income, in 1864, was $111.45; which was divided among the schools as heretofore, in the same manner as the yearly appropriations by the town.

And now we have the "Bullock Fund" of $5000. carefully invested, and its yearly income, by the terms of the Legacy, to be divided in like manner. It yielded, in 1864, $438.65.

The first action of the town, in relation to the subject before us, was a vote, taken in 1767 "to lease out the *school land.*" Two years later it was voted " to sell the *school land* for as much as it will sell for; the principal to be a fund for schools, and the interest to be applied yearly to pay for schooling." This same year the town raised £3. "in addition to the school interest, to hire schooling the present year." The Treasurer, also, charges himself this year with £7 : 10s., lawful money, which the Quarter Sessions gave the town for schooling;" and two orders are drawn upon him to pay school teachers. As these are the first documents of the kind we find in "the chest," one of them is here inserted.

To Mr. PETER WOODBURY, Town Treasuser:

Please to pay to Simeon Chamberlain, the sum of eighteen shillings, it being for two weeks schooling last February and March: and this shall discharge you for so much.

Royalston, September ye 19th. 1769.

£0 : 18 : 0.	Benjamin Woodbury, Peter Woodbury.	} Select Men.

The next year, Capt. John Fry is found exercising still another honorable office, and draws from the town treasury, £2 : 10. for five weeks school-teaching. The same year, John Crawford draws £2. for one month, Simeon Chamberlain £1 : 16s. for one month; and Isaac Esty four shillings for boarding a "School Dame." The next year Hannah Richardson, receives eighteen shillings and eight pence for teaching school four weeks and boarding herself, and Dr. Stephen Bacheller £3. for teaching school seven weeks and boarding himself. In 1777 the town voted that "the school money interest, and security be committed to the town Treasurer.

As yet there were no school houses. The schools were accommodated in the dwellings, and sometimes in the barns of the settlers; but in 1777 an article came before the town, "To see if the town will build a school-house as near the meeting-house in Royalston as convenient, if not, to see [if the town] will give liberty to a number of the inhabitants, near the centre, to build a school-house in said place for their own benefit." The town declined to build, but granted the liberty asked in that alternative. Accordingly a school-house was built near the site of the Sibley house, so called. Tradition has preserved the names of the first three teachers employed in this house. The first was a foreigner, by the name of Wood, whose reputation, as a teacher, long lingered in the memories of his patrons and pupils; and there are those even now who remember that he was esteemed a "very learned man." The second was Ammi Falkner, afterwards deacon; the third Ebenezer Pierce of Warwick, afterwards deacon of the Baptist Church, and father of the late deacon Ebenezer Pierce of this town.

The *districting* of the town proved quite difficult, and was not adjusted till after several abortive experiments. In 1781 the town was divided into six districts. One of these, however,— the south west,—passed from under the jurisdiction of Royalston in 1783, and became a part of Orange, leaving us only five districts,—one in the centre, one in the east, one in the north, and two in the west part of the town.

The town was re-districted in 1795, giving us nine districts, which continued, with little variation, down to 1820. In 1797, as the result of much discussion, it was ' voted to build school-houses in the several school districts; and, that equal justice may be rendered to individuals, as near as possible, voted that the school-houses shall be built as near the centre of the districts as the situation of the inhabitants and the roads will admit, and that each district may agree on the spot. Voted to choose a committee to lay before the town an estimate of the expense of building the several school-houses; and, where there are houses built that in their opinion will answer the purpose, to see how they can agree with the proprietors for them; likewise to report the dimensions and method of finishing.' The committee consisted of Capt. Jon'n. Sibley, Mr. Benj. Hutchinson, and Capt. Peter Woodbury, who reported Feb. 2d, 1797.

The plan of six of these houses was as follows: 20 by 24ft: 9 1-2ft. stud; square roof; six windows each with 15 7 by 9 lights; the inside walls ceiled; over head crowning and plastered: the seats round the walls on three sides and raised eight inches, and eighteen inches from the walls, with a good writing table before them and a shelf for books beneath; seats before the tables; an entrance way at one end of the house six ft. wide: two doors to enter the room; and the whole to be finished up in workmanlike manner and the outside painted. The three other houses differed only in dimensions. Estimated cost of all, $2,018.

Final action on his report was not reached until May 7th. 1798, when it was adopted and $1500, instead of $2,018, appropriated for the work. A committee, consisting of one from each district, was authorized to carry the same into effect. Three school houses,—that under the hill, that in the north ward, and that in the Arm district,—were found of sufficient value to require an allowance to the proprietors. The result was, that the town secured nine commodious and respectable school-houses. one of which,—that in " the city,"—still remains as a specimen of the rest; while the frames of several others have been wrought into the structures of the present day. The town found, in the end, that the original estimate was nearer right than their appropriation, and had to raise $450. to foot the bills. Since 1820 three new districts have been added; and we now have a round dozen.

The school money of Royalston has generally been divided among the districts by a special committee, annually chosen, and but occasionally instructed. The general result, we believe, has been reasonably satisfactory.

Since manufacturing centres began to control population, and rail-roads have come in to change travel and leave the old centres out in the cold, the common lot of back towns and districts has fallen heavily upon parts of Royalston. Our schools used to be thronged; and middle aged citizens remember when their respective schools numbered 40, 60, 75, and even 100. But now, in these same districts, we have to reverse the scale, and run down from 40, to a dozen, and even less. At the same time in So. Royalston, where then there was no school, they now require two. The last school year their schools, together, numbered 101 in the summer, and 111 in the winter term.

During the first third of the present century, when the school fund yielded only $50, or $60, and the town raised from $300, to $500, a year, quite a number of our nine districts had nearly, or quite, six months' schooling annually. During the school year 1864—65, the schools of Royalston cost the town $1674.29, yielding an aggregate of 67 1-2 months of schooling, or a little more than an average of five months to each of the public schools; and at an average cost of $25. per month. Taking the extremes of our accomplished history, we have in the school year of 1864 —65, the average cost of schooling $25. per month, while in 1770, and 1771, Capt. John Fry keeps school five weeks and boards himself for £2 : 10s.=$8.33 plus; John Crawford, one month for £2.=$6.66, plus; and the next year Dr. Bachellor keeps school seven weeks and boards himself for £3.=$10. Or, if we drop the average in the year 1864—65, and take the highest figures in each period, we have George B. Boyd teaching in So. Royalston for $61. board included, in 1864—65, and Dr. Stephen Bacheller teaching and boarding himself, in 1772 for $5.71 plus; per month. These are rather strong contrasts.

Royalston has neither graded schools, nor High School, within the meaning of the statute. The population is not large enough to bring us within the requisition of the law in the last particular, while the extent of our territory and the issolated condition of our population, prevent or certainly interpose very serious obstacles in the way of grading the schools.

There has prevailed a commendable interest, from the early times, in providing extra schooling for the advanced pupils. A fall school, of a high order, has usually been kept in the middle of the town, sustained in part by tuition fees, and the balance made up by subscriptions. Several terms of a similar character have been well sustained in So. Royalston.

The supervision of the Public schools of Royalston presents much the same history as in other towns. At first the ministers were expected to look after this matter. By and by the town came into the practice to choose a committee to 'join with the ministers in this office, but without expense to the tax-payers.' Sometimes this arrangement contributed to the amusement, if not the edification of the schools; teachers and scholars taking upon themselves to be quite officious in furnishing the "committee men" with books, especially when the "parsing class" was called out. The shrewder part were sure to leave their *spectacles* at home, but occasionally the whisper would go round "He's got his book wrong side up," and the like. And the speech-making was often rich. But after all, we have sometimes been led to ask, " Take it all in all, were there not some rare and far-reaching elements for good, in the old way, that have unhappily fallen out of the new?"

One of the measures by which we judge of the general status of a community, with respect to education, is found in the number of those who pass through the Public schools, and means of culture at home, up to the college, the professional schools, and into the learned professions. We close this note with the record of Royalston, in one of these particulars,—the native-born of the town, who have graduated from College. We designate the deceased as usual, and those who devoted themselves to teaching, or business without a profession by the †.

*George Newton, Esq.	Graduated	Dartmouth	—
*†Franklin Jones	"	Amherst	1829
Rev. Sidney Holman	"	Williams	1830
*Rev. Sylvester Davis	"	—	—
His Ex'y Alexander H. Bullock	"	Amherst	1836
*Prof. Nelson Wheeler	"	Yale	1836
Rev. Jesse K. Bragg		Amherst	1838
†Stephen Holman,		Williams	1839
Rev. Ariel E. P. Perkins	"	Amherst	1840
Hosea Davis,	"	Dartmouth	1842
†C. B. Metcalf,	"	Yale	1842
Rev. Amory Gale	"	Brown Un'y	1843
†George B. Newton	"	Yale	1843
*Leonard L. Leathe	"	Amherst	1843
Rev. Ebenezer Cutler,	"	Un'y of Vt.,	1845
Rev. Henry Cummings.	"	Amherst	1847
Hon. Benjamin C. Perkins, Esq.	"	Dartmouth	1848
*Benjamin S. H. Brown	"	Harvard Un'y	1850
J. Ormond Wilson	"	Dartmouth	1850
Samuel C. Gale, Esq.	"	Yale	1854
Charles A. Gregory, Esq.	"	Harvard Un'y	1865
†Henry M. Harrington	"	Amherst	1860
†Charles G. G. Paine	"	"	1861
Rev. Albert Bryant	"	"	1862

Several natives of Royalston entered college, but, for various reasons, did not complete their course.

Rev. David Shepardson, nearly completed the full course.

Rev T. Willard Lewis left college at the close of his 3d year.

*Dr. Daniel C. Perkins was 2 1-2 years in college.

*Rufus Henry Bullock one year.

*Ephraim Richardson had nearly or quite completed his college course, when he died.

We mention last the Rev. Ammi Nichols, son of Dea. Isaac Nichols, born in town, 1781. Tho' he graduated at no college he obtained a good education, passed through a regular course of Theological study under the instruction of Rev. Asa Burton, D. D., of Thetford, Vermont, and has been in the ministry for more than 60 years.

NOTE C.—PAGE 60.   LONGEVITY IN ROYALSTON.

The following list of Royalston men and women, who have died at an advanced age, has been made up, in good part, by researches among our grave yards. But many a grave has no headstone to tell aught of its occupant; and not a few headstones have lost the power of utterance. These facts, together with the recollections still lingering among us of *very aged persons*, of " the days of whose years," there remains neither record nor monument, assure us that our list is far from complete.

It may be remarked that the longevity of the people of Royalston has been as remarkable within the last generation, as in the earlier days. In 1837, five persons died aged respectively 85, 86, 87, 88, 94. In 1840, five persons died aged 82, 85, 87, 96, 96. In 1843, we have 80, 81, 84, 84, 88, 89. In 1849,—82, 86, 88, 89, 96. In 1850,—86, 88, 89, 91, 94. The next year, —82, 86, 90, 90, 96. In 1856,—80, 80, 85, 88, 88. In 1859, —81, 82, 83, 85, 85, 85. In 1864,—81, 91, 93.

Age 105 yrs. Mrs. Susannah Carpenter.
" 98 " David Mead.
" 97 " Lois Eager, Ruth Bliss.
" 96 " Sarah Beal, Benjamin Hutchinson, Aaron Bliss, Betsey Cozens.
" 95 " John Fry.
" 94 " Alice Clement, Mary Bullock.
" 93 " Mrs. Henry Peck, Wm. Ellis, Jonas Allen, Martha Davis, Lydia Walker.
" 92 " Elizabeth Allen, Benj. Eddy, Anna Hale Bliss, Rebekah Sibley, Squier Davis.
" 91 " Thomas Perry, Samuel Felch, David Cook, Tamer Bliss, Geo. Coffin, Robert Thompson.
" 90 " Wm. Brewer, Mrs. Wm. Brewer, Obadiah Walker, Jon'n Cutler, Esther Hill, Nathan Bliss.
" 89 " Mary Waite, Ruth Beal, Hannah Perry, Simeon Stockwell.
" 88 " Jon'n Bosworth, Mrs. Aaron Grant, Joel Miles, Sophia Raymond, Nathan Reed, Sally Stockwell, Henry Nichols, Hope R. Hale, Mary Bacheller, Mary Holman.
" 87 " Timothy Richardson, Mrs. Joseph Stockwell, Mrs Hewes, Mrs. Joseph Emerson, Mrs. Richardson, Mehitable Clark, Mary Felch, Elizabeth Kendall, Marsilvia Chase.
" 86 " Sarah Green, Jonas Allen, Rebekah Black, Mrs. John Fry, Joseph Stockwell, Mrs. Ellis, Silas Bowker, Mrs. Smith, Sarah Waite, Thomas Beal, Joseph Emerson, Sarah Hubbard, Elizabeth Richardson, David Fisher, Susey Allen, Betsey Hale.
" 85 " Mrs. Shumway, Mrs. Blanchard, Martha Davis, Hugh Bullock, Silas Chubb, Elizabeth Bennet, Ruth Estabrook, Elijah Nichols, Rebekah Ken-

dall, Polly Clement, Lois Goodard, Hannah
Estabrook.
Age 84 yrs. Mary Town, Mrs. Ezekial Cutler, Mrs. Maclellan,
Elizabeth Cutler, Reuben Walker, Amos Jones,
Mary Pierce, Eunice Felton, Enoch Whitmore,
Sarah Chase, Ebenezer Chase, Sophia Davis.
Stephen Richardson.
" 83 " Henry Nichols, Mrs. Holman, Moses Maclellan.
Stephen Bacheller, Asahel Davis.
" 82 " Samuel Felch, Moses Pratt, Timothy Richardson,
Mary Hutchinson, Mrs. Cummings, Thos. Blodgett, Mary Emerson, Hannah Thurston, Nathan
B. Newton, Judah Stockwell, Becca Pratt, Sarah Chamberlain, John Burbank, Asa Walker.
" 81 " Rogers Chase, Thankful Blanchard, Josiah Piper,
Alexander Parkman Davis, Sarah Bragg, Shubel Blanding, Elizabeth Leach, Daniel Woodbury, Moses Garfield, Deborah Davis, Willard
Newton.
" 80 " Mrs. Bosworth, Mrs. Poor, Mrs. Nichols, Mrs.
Shepardson, William Town, Mehitable Nichols,
Nathan Cutting, Josiah Hicks, Mehitable Allen,
Paul Church, Joshua Hewes, Elijah Walker,
Esther Hill, Mary Moore, Daniel Shepardson,
Percis Woodbury.

NOTE V.—PAGE 63. INDUSTRIAL PURSUITS AND RESULTS.

Royalston began as an agricultural town; and so continued for half a century. But farmers were then *artisans*, and their families *quasi* manufacturing establishments. They had their shops for stormy days, winter evenings and leisure hours, where they made and mended farming tools and household utensils. The shoeing, of all kinds, was either done at home, or by exchange of labor and skill with some neighboring Crispin, or Smith, who was also a farmer, and turned to his last or forge, as the good housewife to her knitting, only in the intervals of other work. Indeed, almost every thing needful for a plain and substantial life was secured by mutual helpfulness, to the great saving of money, and the greater growth of good neighborhood. Thus there was a common property, so to speak, in the eight saw-mills, four grist-mills, six tanneries, two brick-yards, two potashes, the oil-mill, the clothier's mill, and all the shoe-shops, smithies, cider-mills, &c. &c., of the town. And as the farmers raised and dressed flax, a flax-break a swingling-knife, and a hatchel were as necessary in the outfit of a barn, or a hovel, as a pitchfork, or a flail. Sugar and molasses were home-made; and he was accounted a poor farmer who could not make sap-taps, troughs and buckets, or who would not spend time enough among the rock-maples, in the Spring weeks, to supply his family.

But madam, also, and the girls were something more than house-keepers. They had their *factory chamber* from whence the hum of the big and the little wheel, and the click of the shuttle, told of active brains and skillful fingers on the other side of the house, and of a thrift, within doors, rightfully claiming equal partnerships in the concern. Woolens and linens from these chambers had no taint of shoddy about them, and, when made up into garments by the same hands that carded, spun and wove them, they wore as though seam, button-hole and fabric vied with each other to put honor on the fair makers. They may not have been as fine in texture, as glossy in surface, or in cut as stylish, as those of to-day; but they had the breath of home in them—were comfortable and durable, putting no one in mortal fear of rip, or rent, on the slightest occasion—no one who wore them, so far as we learn, ever went to jail to pay wife or mother, daughter or sister, for his wardrobe; and in those days, it required no city tailor, or Parisian mantua maker, to get up a man or a woman.

Is it any wonder the young people early went in for these simple, but sound, corporations, the basis of whose Stock was strong hands and willing hearts?—any wonder, either, that these enterprises, encumbered neither by *silent* partners nor *fancy* stock, seldom proved a misadventure? All the elements of success were intrinsic with the parties, and mutual interests, well trained and ripened by early experience, made the toil and care of achieving it no ungrateful task.

Hence new farms, and productive centres sprang up as by magic, bringing the town forward rapidly. Royalston soon began to export, not her people or her forests, as in later days, but the products of agriculture,—grain, beef, pork, mutton and poultry. These the farmers marketed themselves, taking them to Boston, and the lower towns, on their own teams, and bringing back such family stores as were necessary, and the balance in good lawful money, wherewith to pay their taxes, replace log-cabins with frame-houses, enlarge their farms, and settle off the children. Other articles were often added,—a little surplus of wool, of dressed flax, yarn or thread, sometimes a web of woolen or linen cloth—a little maple sugar, and often some wooden notions, wrought in leisure hours by the cunning Yankee farmer, or his boys. All these were stowed in the wagon, or sleigh; found ready sale in the market, and helped to swell the incomes of the forefathers. The tanneries frequently produced more leather than was needed for home consumption, and the surplus was sent off to the market. And good honest leather it was, too, *tanned* after the old style, and not *cooked* in boiling extract, and the *scraps* glued together for sole-leather. The potashes, too, wrought in the common course; and William Jerrel, the hatter, bore a hand in keeping the balance of trade in favor of the town. Him we must pause to commemorate, so far at least, as to state, that liberty was granted him, in 1780, to build a hatter's shop upon the public square, and occupy the ground so long as he continued the hatter's business thereon. For many years he furnished the people with hats, and became also their *factor* in the fur trade, thus in more ways than one, making himself quite an acquisition to the town. There was another hatter in the neighborhood of Lawrence falls; but we suspect that he found little encouragement, for, departing our limits, he left not even his name behind him. But there was a *clothier* in that vicinity, one Benjamin May, who did the town good service. He built first at the base of the great Falls, but soon after moved up stream, to, or near, the site of Amos Doane's unique concern, where he scoured and fulled the home-mades of the people. His business passed into the hands of Joel Nourse, about the begining of the present century. Mr. Nourse built the dam north of the red pail-shop; erected a blacksmith-shop, in which he ran a trip hammer, and a nail-cutting machine, and got under his control the oil-mill, the clothier's mill, and about all the business of the neighborhood. This was the first considerable movement, looking toward innovation in our industrial pursuits. It soon however ceased to be alarming; and our first half-century closed with the agricultural *star* riding high, and unchallenged, in the ascendant.

But since then the times have changed, and Royalston has changed with them. Farming is no longer regnant; while the division of labor is carried out so sharply, and the competitions of mechanics, manufactures and tradesmen is so close, that it is vain to attempt any thing but farming in the country; and we must drive off to the *centers* of business out of town, for the supply of almost every earthly want. Our shoe-shops, smithies, grist-mills and cider-mills, have fallen into the *dual* number; while our oil-mill, clothier's mill, carding-mill, hatter's shop, trip-hammer nail-machine, potashes, brick-yards, and tanneries have all, and utterly disappeared. And so have the *factory chambers*, and all (of inanimate make and mould) that once graced them, is packed away in the attic, if not long since consigned to the flames. We shall never again give the Commonwealth a Governor who will ' remember to have passed, in early evening, to the sweet sleep of childhood under the æolian cadence of the spinning-wheel.'

But saw-mills have multiplied under this great industrial change. We have now thirteen, and all supplied with modern appliances for converting our forests into lumber, or else stock for wooden ware; while hard by them are the shops in which a portion of this stock is made into pails, chairs, brush-woods, boxes shoe-pegs, and numerous other articles of merchandise. The residue of the stock is sent out of town, by car and wagon-loads, to more capacious manufactories.

The statistics, returned to the Secretary's Office for the last year, report 1.440.000 feet of lumber prepared for the market; 280 cords of staves and 50 M. of shingles; chair stock got out to the value of $5.650; 32.000 chairs made in town; 36.000 pails. $10.866 worth of brush-woods; 6.000 bushels of shoe-pegs; $12.000 worth of other wooden wares; 1.585 cords of fire-wood and bark prepared for the market, and 200 bushels of charcoal; all of which runs up an aggregate of $86.556.

The fathers lived *in* the forests; their children live *off* of them. We are getting out of the woods, and 'a man is famous, according as he lifts up axes upon the thick trees'—certainly a man is accounted *rich* as he *has thick trees* upon which to lift up axes.

Manufacturing has been essayed at several points since the begining of the last half century." Dea. Joseph Sawyer, by diverting the waters of Little Pond from their natural out-let, and leading them around, by means of a canal, to the hollow, north of the common, procured water-power for his cabinet-shop, in which he, and, after him, Dea. Seth Holman and his son, Seth N. Holman, continued, till quite recently, the manufacture of Pine Furniture. A dam was built below this shop, and upon it a wheel-wright, and carriage shop erected, in which some business was done for a time. Neither of these water powers are now used; and we see no good reason why the natural out-let of Little Pond should not be re-opened and its waters, no longer in bondage to man, allowed to run singing along in their primeval and romantic channel, down to Long Pond and the classic Tully.

And we should like to see the now useless, unseemly, and unhealthy canal filled up.

The wheel-wright shop is now used by the Messrs Chas. H. and Phineas S. Newton as a Palm Leaf shop. The last year they prepared 18,000 pounds of Leaf, and put it out to be braided into Hats, notch-braid, and woven into Shaker Webs and Binds. The estimated value of the Palm Leaf businesss, carried on in town, is $12,000.

After Joel Nourse left town, Benjamin Bragg became proprietor of his privilege, and continued awhile the clothier's business. He added machinery for wool-carding and afterwards engaged in the manufacturing of Satinets. He was burned out in 1850; since which time the neighborhood of the Falls has furnished no manufacturing business except such as is connected with the sawmill and pail-shop.

"The Royalston Cotton and Wool Manufacturing Company" was incorporated in 1813. Eight persons were named in the Act. The company erected a Mill on the site now occupied by the Woolen Mill at So. Royalston. We understand that the company was not very successful. One member after another sold out, and the whole concern came into the hands of Silas Coffin and Rufus Bullock. This Mill was burned in 1833; and Mr. Bullock became the sole proprietor of the privilege, and the property appertaining thereto. The next year he built the Stone Mill, still standing; put in four sets of woolen machinery, and continued to run them till his decease. Hon. George Whitney is now the proprietor—has expended a good deal of money in additions and improvements, and, according to the statistics of the town, for the last year, there were 160,877 pounds of scoured wool worked up in the mill, producing 166,673 yards of cassimere, valued at $233,346.

Since the starting of this second Mill, So. Royalston has been steadily pushing on upon the rising scale. It is now securely established as the center and seat of Royalston business. Miller's river here makes one of its graceful bends, just as though intent on giving us a goodly stretch of water-power; and here also the Rail-Road strikes us just at the fitting place. Thus are blended the two great powers, which, in modern times, rule and control both business and population. We indicate the result, thus far by the following statement. In 1833 So. Royalston contained 10 dwelling houses, a saw and grist mill, and a factory in ashes. Now, the factory, risen, Phenix-like, from its ashes, stands at the head of thronging mills, shops, and business operations, while two meeting-houses, two stores, a depot, public house, livery-stable, and 78 dwelling houses, justify So. Royalston, in claiming to be catalogued among the vigorous and promising New England villages.

We add the statistics of agriculture from the same report. 163 farms small and great; 8,220 bushels of grain of all kind; 15,760 bushels of vegetables; 2,429 tons of hay; 1,053 neat cattle; 435 sheep; 207 horses; 115 swine; income from poultry and eggs sold $580; value of honey $288; value of maple sugar $1,400.

NOTE W.—PAGE 66.   BURIAL GROUNDS.

Of these there are nine in town, besides family yards, and places where one, or only a few bodies have been interred.

The original burial ground was projected by the Proprietors, and occupied the east side of the public square. Several interments were made on this ground; but being found very unsuitable for the purpose, it was exchanged for a lot lying south-west of the original plot, and on the south side of the Athol road. Subsequently the town added some acres to this lot and enclosed the whole with a stone wall. It has also a receiving tomb and a hearse-house fronting upon the road; and hither, from year to year, for more than a century, have many of the dead of Royalston been borne to their last sleep.

A small yard was early inclosed near the first Baptist meeting house, and numbers of the forefathers were buried there; but it now lieth waste, and the forest usurps the field of the dead. Our centennial Poet gathered one of his Garlands from this 'grave yard below the hill.'

A family lot lies nearly opposite the residence of Mr. Nathan Bliss, just east of "the city." Here are the graves of his ancestors, and some of his own family, with *but a* step between the habitation of the living and the dead.

North-west from here, and near the line of Richmond, is still another early grave yard; and occasionally even now some relict of the original families of this neighborhood makes dying request to be buried there, by the side of kindred dust; but, with the exception of one or two family inclosures, this field also lieth waste, and the traces of former care for these ancient graves are fast being obliterated.

Another field of graves, well walled, having a receiving tomb, and still frequented by the solemn processions, lies upon a commanding eminence near the Warwick line, and south west from the old Baptist common. The public road used to wind up by this yard; but, since it was *turned* and carried to the foot of the hill, this burial place is less accessible.

Still another congregation of the dead is found on the original farm of Ephraim Hill; and long rows of graves tell of the large families that once made this section of the town quite populous.

A small neighborhood grave yard has lately been laid out on the farm of Eri Shepardson, about a mile from the Athol line. It is deeded to the proprietors, well inclosed and thus far neatly kept.

So. Royalston has two yards. The old one lies directly east of the Methodist church, and in the very heart of the village. It is now seldom, if ever, used for burial purposes; and its removal is a matter of debate. To the east of the village, and lying up pleasantly from Miller's river and west of the road here running north, is the new yard, fenced, a receiving tomb on the east side, fronting the road, well kept, and fast filling up with graves. The thing to be regretted about this yard is, that the living tide must ere long sweep over and beyond it, raising the same painful debate, which now exists with respect to the old yard.

Shortly before the decease of Hon. Rufus Bullock, he became much interested in establishing a new cemetery near the middle of the town. Having secured the co-operation of several gentlemen, citizens of the town, a lot was purchased, lying up from the east bank of the Lawrence, and a short distance south of the road leading to So. Royalston, from which an open and good avenue leads to the grounds. The grounds have been fenced, a gate and receiving tomb, fronting the avenue, erected; and the grounds themselves partially laid out, and some little work done upon them. But the original plan, in respect to the ground, still remains to be carried out by the legal proprietors. It will be seen that Mr. Bullock, who was suddenly removed by death while this work was in progress, provided by his will, in case the town accepted of his legacy—see *Sixteenth Item*—for the proper care of this cemetery, *when established*. The town has accepted of the legacy, and thereby become the custodian of the fence, gate, receiving tomb, and the ground, "to keep the same, or cause them to be kept, in a good state of repair, that is to say, to maintain in *good order* and *condition* the said ground, fence, gate and receiving tomb." We have no doubt, the town as soon as the grounds are *once put in good order* and *condition*, will sacredly fulfil this trust, and keep faith with him, whose body now rests from its labors in the spot he had already in part prepared for it ere he was called away.

Hitherto there had been no measures adopted for assuring those who "fall asleep" that their graves, their monuments, and their surroundings, should have safe and sacred keeping. One isolated field of graves after another has been given over to desolation, and the same fate seems little else than a question of time with respect to the rest. It is no pleasant anticipation of the living, though powerfully suggested by passing events, that future generations may stumble upon their graves among the pastures and woodlands, or that their monuments may be endangered by the "loging" operations of an enterprising future. Hence it is no wonder that anxiety is felt, to look up the title deeds, if there be any, and provide if possible, for some better keeping of the grave yards.

There has been one instance in Royalston, and but one, to our knowledge, of grave-robbing. In July of 1823, Mr. Jarvis Weeks, while passing through the belt of woods, which skirts the southeast shores of Little Pond, came upon a newly made booth, which excited his suspicions. He called upon Mr. Peter Woodbury, and returned with him to make examination. They found a grave-robe, and fragments of a human body. Going thence to the grave-yard they found cause to suspect that the newly made grave of Daniel Forbes had been disturbed. It was opened, and the body was not there. At this time several medical students were studying with Dr. Bacheller. Two of these were arrested; and two made good their escape. A set of human bones, lately prepared, was found in the possession of one of the former. His companion turned State's evidence; in process of time he was convicted of disinterring the body of Daniel Forbes, and due penalty awarded him.

This outrage produced great excitement, and for a long time the new graves were watched with painful anxiety.

A brother of Daniel Forbes, gathered up the bones that had been thus feloniously taken from their grave, and secretly buried them in the yard below the hill, carefully concealing all indications of their locality.

THE OLD BURYING GROUND.

BY WHITTIER.

Our vales are sweet with fern and rose,
    Our hills are maple crowned;
But not from these our fathers chose
    The village burying ground.

The dreariest spot in all the land
    To death they set apart;
With scanty grace from Nature's hand,
    With none from that of Art.

A winding wall of mossy stone,
    Frost-flung and broken, lines
A lone acre thinly grown,
    With grass and wandering vines.

Unshaded smites the Summer sun,
    Unchecked the Winter blast;
The school-girl learns the place to shun,
    With glances backward cast.

For thus our fathers testified—
    That he might read who ran—
The emptiness of human pride,
    The nothingness of man.

They dared not plant the grave with flowers,
    Nor dress the funeral sod,
When, with a love as deep as ours,
    They left their dead with God.

ELIZABETH LADY TEMPLE.

Royalston has had at least one *titled* land holder. Lady Temple, widow of Sir John Temple, baronet, once owned 800 acres of our soil. There is lying before us a deed of two 200 hundred acre lots,—Nos. 39 and 40—running to Squier Davis, with her Ladyship's signature subscribed. There is also a letter, from Thomas S. Winthrop, addressed to Henry Goddard, recorded vol. I. page 63, (supplement) of the town's Records, appointing the said Goddard agent for Lady Temple, to pay her annual taxes on two other 200 acre lots—Nos. 37, and 57, and to "take particular care that no trespass be committed on said lots."

All of these lots were originally drawn by John Erving Esq., but became the property of James Bowdoin, the second Governor of the State of Massachusetts. Upon his decease they were set off, in the division of his estate, to his daughter, Elizabeth, the wife of Sir John Temple.

Her husband was born at Nodde's Island, (now East Boston,) but belonged to one of the most ancient families of the English nobility; founded, it is claimed, by Leofric, Earl of Mercia,—

"——that grim Earl, who ruled
In Coventry;"

and who married—

"The woman of a thousand summers back, Godiva,"

celebrated in one of Tennyson's poems.

Lord Palmerston, late Premier of Great Britian, was of the same Saxon family, and even as simple Henry John Temple, could look down upon all the Normandy descended nobles of the realm.

Sir John was some time Lieut. Governor of the Province of New Hampshire. Afterward he became the eighth English Baronet of his name. He was also made Baronet of Nova Scotia. He was Surveyor General of Customs in England and held other honorable offices under the crown, when, in 1774, on account of becoming implicated with Dr. Franklin in exposing the perfidious plots of the royal government against the chartered rights and just liberties of the American colonies in general, and Massachusetts in particular, he was dismissed, on the same day with Franklin, from all office. He thus lost a thousand pounds sterling, per annum; but kept a good conscience, and a bright Whig record; while he endeared himself to all true lovers of liberty and public honor.

It is grateful to find our *titled* proprietress deriving her dignity from so staunch a friend of the American cause; and not less grateful to know that Lady Temple proved herself every way worthy of the ancient and noble family in which once shone that bright particular star, the Lady Godiva, of Coventry memory.

It will discover but the ordinary weakness of human nature if we make a further note of the legitimate pretensions of Royalston.

John Hancock, the first Governor of our State, and for twelve years our Chief Magistrate, was also, it will be remembered, a large proprietor in our soil, holding 11 of the original *lots* in his own individual right, and being joint partner in all the common and undivided lands of the town. And now we see that James Bowdoin, the second Governor of the State of Massachusetts, was also a proprietor in our town. Thus our first two Chief Magistrates, if not native born, or bred, were land-holders and tax-payers in Royalston. Add now, that his Excellency, our present Governor, is both Royalston born and bred, and we may rejoice in the promise, "And their nobles shall be of themselves; and their Governor shall proceed from the midst of them."

PUBLIC GATHERINGS.

The location of Royalston would not suggest large conventions of the people; nevertheless such things have happened here, and with never a failure.

The town has witnessed three musters,—one in 1811, or 12, one in 1823, and one in 1829. But with a resident Major General, near a dozen Colonels, several Majors, and at least a score of live Captains, it is no wonder that some of those old gala-days found welcome even in this out-post of Worcester County.

But *the* gathering was reserved for 1840, during the Log-cabin canvass. Through the kindness of D. A. Goddard, Esq., of the Worcester Spy, we have been favored with the copy of a brilliant report of the day, published in the Boston Atlas at the time,—from which, and our own reminiscences, we briefly sketch the occasion.

The Whig Association of Royalston had invited General Wilson, of Keene, to address them on Saturday, May 30th, of that famous year. Notice had been posted in no few of the adjacent towns; and the Royalston Whigs soon ascertained that *the people* would be upon them in force, resolved to convert their little town affair into a pageant. They set themselves to prepare for the emergency, built a cabin of white birch logs, and an awning of green boughs; and had all things arranged in good time. At sun-rise, Saturday morning, the national flag was displayed above the platform; and, at the firing of a heavy gun in the distance, a fine company of mounted Whig Voters of Royalston, under the command of Capt. John Whitmore, rode rapidly northward to receive the Fitzwilliam artillery, who were on their march to do escort duty to their old General. Thus reinforced they took the Keene road, received the General, and a rich brass band from Keene, with military salute, and conducted them to their quarters. Captain Whitmore and his company then rode south, and soon returned, escorting, the united lines of Petersham, Barre, Phillipston and Athol to the common. It was a triumphal procession of carriages, one mile and a half in length, some of the vehicles containing from 20 to 30 men, and well appointed with bands, whose music filled the air. Then came in the line from the east, in which were united the stout and true whigs of Hubbardston, Templeton, Gardner, and Winchendon, inspired by music, and their carriages refreshed with abundance of green boughs. Any fiend of the administration, who watched the appearances, must have had some of the apprehensions that struggled in the breast of poor *Macbeth*, when, in the hour of his overthrow, he saw the revengeful army approaching *Dunsinane* with branches of the *Birnam* wood waving over them :

  —— " and now a wood
  Comes towards Dunsinane."

This line was more than a mile in length. One carriage from Winchendon contained a small army of seventy whig voters; another from Templeton was crowded with fifty.

Pictorial insignia, with telling mottoes, illustrated the banners, —those *proof sheets* of the coming elections.

Thus gathered the people from abroad; while the Whigs of Royalston, men, women and children, all holding themselves personally responsible for the success of the day, made up the thousands, who thronged the common, marched through the Log-Cabin, and gathered, at least 3000 strong, before the platform, a little past noon, to listen to their chosen leaders—Hon. Rufus Bullock presided as President of the Day, and Col. Benjamin Brown acted as Chief Marshal. Messrs Lee and Mason of Templeton, Stevens of Athol, Parkhurst of Petersham, Bryant of Barre, Davenport of Mendon, and Alex. H. Bullock of Royalston, spoke briefly, but happily of Whig principles, and Whig prospects. They were often interrupted by the enthusiastic cheers of the audience, and the deep-toned cannon.

General Wilson followed; and for two hours and a quarter beguiled his hearers of all consciousness, except that of the presence of the Orator, his eloquence, his theme.

An abundant entertainment of crackers, cider, cheese and accompaniments, closed the day, all the doings of which had been marked by the richest enthusiasm of that exciting canvass, which bore " Tippacanoe and Tyler too ", to an overwhelming victory.

WARNING OUT OF TOWN.

Under the early laws the last *legal settlement* of any person, laid the town, wherein it was effected, liable for his support and the support of his family should they come to want. Such settlement was secured by peaceable residence within the limits of a town. As a precautioning measure, therefore, the towns were allowed a *veto* on new comers; and the Selectmen might issue their precept to any constable of the town to *warn out* such persons from their limits. The effect of this process was to prevent a legal settlement, whether the warnings were obeyed or not. To make this system the more effective no citizen might harbor persons or families from abroad without giving written notice to the selectmen setting forth the names, the last settlement, and the pecuniary *Status* of the same.

As this *warning* affected neither the rights nor interests of those upon whom it was served, except in this particular only, it became the practice of many towns to make a clean thing of it, and serve the injunction upon all alike, who came to town to reside.

Several pages of our records are taken up with these proceedings, and the names of persons who afterwards became prominent citizens, and established very respectable families, are found under this *ban*. We find no instance in which those, who were warned to "depart the limits of the town within fifteen days," heeded the mandate. After the change of the Poor Laws, this rather hard looking process ceased to be practiced.

We give a single example of *warning out*, suppressing names merely.

"WORCESTER, ss. To either of the Constables of the town of Royalston in the county of Worcester; GREETING.

You are, in the name of the Commonwealth of Massachusetts, directed to warn and notify ——— ———, wife and children, who lately came into this town of Royalston for the purpose of abiding therein, not having obtained the town's consent, that they depart the limits thereof in fifteen days from the date hereof: and of this precept, with your doings hereon, you are to make return into the Office of the Town Clerk of Royalston in twenty days next coming, that such further proceedings may be had thereon as the laws direct.

Given under our hands and seals at Royalston" &c.
WORCESTER, ss. Royalston, ———.

In obedience to this precept I have warned and given notice to ——— ———, and his, to depart the limits of this town of Royalston, by leaving an attested copy of this precept at their last and usual place of abode.

——— ———, Constable for Royalston.
ATTEST: ——— ———, Town Clerk of Royalston.

PERSECUTION OF THE BIRDS.

Royalston, in common with other towns, for a long time joined in this cruel business, setting a price on the heads of some, and giving up all to the mercy of men and boys with shotted guns in their hands. The bounty for an old crow was 25cts., for a young one half that sum, and for a crow-black bird 6 1-4cts. The victims were to be brought to the authorities "to have their heads cut off." Later the scale of bounties was reduced, and at length the black bird was let off. The town, also, paid bounties only to the inhabitants, and for birds killed within their own limits, requiring the recipients to make oath in the premises.

In 1818, about the time the property qualification for voting was taken off, the General Court began to legislate for the protection of the birds; but, feeling their way into a new era, they left it with the town to decide annually whither the bird-laws should be enforced within their limits. This gave the champions of the birds, so far as they had any, the opportunity to plead their cause each year, and call their fellow citizens to show their hand by open vote. Royalston held to her old faith many years, voting to suspend the operation of the said laws, another, and still another year. And here, too, long continued the old fashioned " hunting-matches," which usually came off on Election Day,—a fearful Bartholomew Day for the poor birds, which were pitilessly shot down in orchard, grove and forest, to swell the quotas of the " match."

It was not only a rational and convenient thing in itself, but it proved beneficent in respect to the feathered tribes, when the date of our political year was transferred from the last Wednesday of May to the first Wednesday of January, since which time this annual onslaught upon the birds has gradually been given up. Indeed wiser and better counsels have now become dominant; and the birds are not only tolerated, but their many virtues are conceded. Many love them for their beauty and their songs; and more, perhaps, cordially accept of them as their natural and most efficient ally against the vandal hordes of insects, whose ravages are the terror of farmer and orchardist.

OBSOLETE TOWN OFFICERS.

Several of the early municipal offices have nearly, or quite, gone out of date. The *Reeves*, once annually elected with all gravity, are now seldom brought forward in the town house, except to make the people sport. Deer long since departed the limits of the town; and as they no longer require a *Steward* to look after them the office of *Deer-Reeve* is practically abolished. While the old style of swine was in vogue, and the question of letting them " run at large, ringed and yoked as the law directs," or restricting them to the liberty of the yard only, *Hog-Reeves* held no despicable office, and their post was no sinecure. But since more tractable breeds have been introduced, which, with moderate keeping, cannot *run at large* however the town may vote, *Hog-Reeves*, like Othello, find their occupation gone. At all events, they are now seldom chosen, unless it be for the fun of the thing, or in compliment to some radiant benedict of the last year.—Field-Drivers and Pounds, also, have mostly died out, and gone to the "pale realms of shades;" while Tithing-men, Stocks, and Whipping-Posts " are known and feared no more." We offer no definitive reason for the last facts,—whether because there are no longer side-seats and galleries in the meeting house wherein to put the Tithing-men, no recess under the pulpit in which to store the stocks, and no pump on the common to which to bind those that deserve chastisement,—because, like the Deer, all the naughty ones have departed the limits of the town, or because it is less popular than formerly to have wholesome oversight and discipline administered. There are those among us, however, who well remember—perhaps have good cause to remember—the Tithing-men. There are those, too, that remember the Stocks, which, when not in use, found storage under the pulpit, and that the town pump was sometimes used for a Whipping-Post. The last case of this kind is still within the memory of the living. The whipping was done upon the body of a light fingered fellow, who had appropriated certain articles from Shubel Blanding's clothes-yard. He was caught and Blanding had the satisfaction not only of receiving his stolen property; but of seeing the thief well *lashed* to the pump, and *take* the line after quite a different fashion, than when he fingered the clothes-line. Those who have always found it all right with their clothes-lines, may think it a fine thing no longer to have a whipping-post; but we have seen some very respectable ladies, even, after returning with an empty basket from the clothes line they left so full the day before, look, and talk too, for all the world, as though they might enjoy just such another sight, as did Mr. Blanding's heart good in the case above recited—But that don't prove it right, to be sure.

THE BLEEDERS.—BY JOHN N. BARTLETT.

Mrs. Margaret Bacheller, wife of Dea. John Bacheller and mother of Mrs. Hannah Bartlett, was an immediate descendant of the Appleton family of Ipswich,—a family remarkable for the manifestation and transmission, by some of its members, of an anomalous physical organization, subjecting the persons so constituted to an extreme liability to bleed profusely from their arteries and veins, upon the occasion of even slight wounds. Hence they are called " Bleeders."

This phenomenon may be thus briefly and accurately described. A cut, or other hurt upon them, assumes at first the common appearance; soon however, if inclined to bleed, a cone of co-agulated blood forms upon the rupture. This cone has a minute apeture, and is large or small according to the wound. After a week or more, as the case may be, the blood begins and continues to flow from the cone in a stream, or more moderately, sometimes for several days in succession perhaps, until that fluid becomes nearly as colorless as water. At this stage the sufferer, if he survives, assumes a most ghastly appearance and is frequently unable to raise a hand or even a finger.

The bleeding ceases when the cone, which becomes very fetid, falls off; a patient surviving this point usually recovers rapidly.

It is found practically useless to stop the flow of blood at the cone, as the continued flow, or pressure internally, would result in death. They often bleed profusely at the nose, and many of them have died from the slightest wounds.

This hemorrhage is said to have first appeared in the Appleton family, who introduced it here from England. None but *males* are bleeders, and the sons of bleeders are *never* subject to it; but a bleeder's daughter, and grand daughter on the mother's side may have sons so predisposed. The number of progenitors, however, who thus resemble their grandfathers, is comparatively small. Eight only of Mrs. Bacheller's descendants are known to the writer, (who is himself an immediate descendant.) as having exhibited this remarkable feature.

Mrs. Bacheller had two brothers, Thomas and Oliver Swain, both of them professional physicians, and both of whom died from excessive bleeding from trivial causes. The eight descendants, above mentioned, were three sons, one grandson, three great grandsons, and one of the fourth generation; three of whom are now living. One of the sons, Thomas, while in the act of making a pen, accidentally penetrated the skin upon the end of his thumb with the point of the knife. The rupture was too slight, however, to have attracted the least attention from an ordinarily constituted person. But, in about two weeks, a cone (the certain precursor of bleeding) began to form, and a hemorrhage soon followed from which he nearly lost his life. At another time a very slight wound upon his foot resulted similarly. Benjamin, another son, bled nearly to death several times from similar slight causes. Chauncy Bartlett, the grandson, (a son of Ira Bartlett,) when about four years old, fell and hit his forehead, slightly rupturing the skin; a hurt which would have ordinarily received no care or attention; but which, in his case, resulted in death by bleeding, in a few days.

Many other instances might be cited, and names given, of persons, near or more remotely connected with the Appletons, having been thus affected. But as the description of one case may be taken as an illustration of all, except in degree, perhaps, it would seem to be a work of supererogation. Science and skill have been alike baffled in the elucidation and treatment of this phenomenon.

DELEGATES,—SENATORS, AND REPRESENTATIVES.

Henry Bond, Delegate to the First Provincial Congress, 1774.
Nahum Green,   "   "   Second   "   "   1774.
Henry Bond,   "   "   Concord Convention for stating Prices,   1779.

Silvanus Hemenway, Delegate to the First Constitutional
    Convention, 1779.
John Fry, his substitute, 1780.
Rufus Bullock, Delegate to the Second and Third Constitu-
    tional Conventions, 1820 & 1853.
John Fry, Delegate at the Ratification of the Constitution
    of U. S. 1788.

Royalston has furnished three Senators, the first of whom died during his first full term: the others served each two terms.

Joseph Estabrook, Esq., Senator, 1828.
Rufus Bullock, Esq., " 1831, & 1832.
Col. George Whitney, " 1863, & 1864.

The first Representative to the General Court, from this town, was chosen May 27, 1766: and at the last town meeting warned in his Majesty's name. The next meeting was called together, Sept. 20th of the same year, but the warrant was issued under the authority of quite a different name, as follows: " In the name of the Government and People of the State of Massachusetts Bay in New England."

After 1776, the town did not send a Representative again till 1780; but thenceforward with a few exceptions, we have a regular succession, generally but one, but sometimes two, annually, down to 1857. Since then, by virtue of the District System, Athol and Royalston alternate. The General Court used to convene annually on the last Wednesday in May,—the old election day —when the Governor and Government elect, for the ensuing year, were inaugurated. In 1831 the political year began in January. Hence, since this change, the *election* of a Representative, as by the Record, does not, as previously, indicate the year of his service—the choice occurring in November, while the member does not take his seat till the first Wednesday of January following. We give the year in which each Representative served.

Timothy Richardson, 1776.
John Fry, 1780, '83, '84, '85, '87.
Peter Woodbury, 1788, '89.
Isaac Gregory, 1794, '95, 1801. 1803, '06 '07, '08.
John Norton, 1800, '13, '14.
Rufus Bullock, 1820, '21, '27. '28, '29.
Benjamin Brown, 1832, '45.
Asahel Davis, 1834.
Arba Sherwin, 1835, '37, 39.
Benjamin Fry, 1838, '40, 54.
Cyrus Davis, 1840.
Barnet Bullock, 1844.
Elmer Newton, 1849.
Tarrant Cutler, 1855.
Joseph Estabrook, 1857.
Elisha F. Brown, 1861.

Jonathan Sibley, 1786.
Oliver Work, 1792.
Philip Sweetzer, 1798.
Joseph Estabrook, 1809, '10. '11, '12, 15, '16, '17, 25.
Squier Davis, 1823.
Stephen Bacheller, Jr. 1826. '30.
Franklin Gregory, 1831, '33.
Russell Morse, 1835, 36, '39.
Benoni Peck, 1836, 1837.
Salmon Goddard, 1838.
Hiram W. Albee, 1843, '46. '52, '53.
Silas Kenney, 1848.
Joseph Raymond, 1850, '51.
Jarvis Davis, 1856.
George Whitney, 1859.
Ebenezer W. Bullard, 1864.

TOWN CLERKS.

John Fry, from 1765 to 1781, with the single exception of 1773, when Dr. Stephen Bacheller was regularly chosen, at the March meeting, and records the doing of the same, as Town Clerk. He signs one other record during the year; but, in some, to us, inexplicable way, John Fry records the May meeting, and affixes his usual "Test" to that, and other records during the year.

Peter Woodbury, 1782, '83, '84, '85, '86, '87, '88, '89, '91, '94.
John Bacheller, 1790, '92, '93.
Daniel Woodbury, 1795, '96.
Isaac Gregory, 1797, ,98, '99, 1800, '06.
Samuel Goddard Jr., 1801, '02.
Joseph Esterbrook, 1804, '05, '08, '09 '10.
Stephen Bacheller Jr. 1807.

John Norton, 1811, '14, '15, '16, '17.
Rufus Bullock, 1812, '13.
Thomas J. Lee, 1818, '21, '22, '23, '24.
Franklin Gregory, 1819, '20, and from 1825 to 1836, inclusive.
Barnet Bullock, from 1837 to 1846, inclusive.
George F. Miller, from 1847 to '51, inclusive.
Joseph Raymond, 1850, '52, '53.
Rufus Henry Bullock, 1854.
Charles H. Newton, from 1855 to 1865, inclusive.

TOWN TREASURERS.

Peter Woodbury, from 1765 to 1770, inclusive.
Silvanus Hemenway, from 1771 to 1777, inclusive.
William Town, 1778, '79, '80,
Jonathan Sibley, from 1781 to 1808, inclusive.
Ebenezer Fry, from 1809 to 1824, inclusive.
Rufus Bullock, from 1825 to 1837, inclusive.
Benjamin Fry, from 1838 to 1554 inclusive, with the exception
    of 1840, when Joseph Esterbrook served.
George Woodbury, from 1855 to 1857, inclusive.
Leonard Wheeler, from 1858 to 1864, inclusive.
Charles H. Newton, 1865.

SELECTMEN.

John Fry, 1765, '67, '68, '71, '72, '80, '91.
Timothy Richardson, 1765, '66, '73, '74, '75, '76, '84, '85.
Benjamin Woodbury, 1765, '66, '69, '73, '74, '75, '76, '77, '78, 81.
Nathan Goddard, 1766.
Isaac Esty, 1767, '68.
Jonathan Sibley, 1767, '68, '77, '78.
Peter Woodbury, 1769, '70, '71, '72, '73, '80, '81, '83, '84, '85,
    '86, '87, '88, '89, '91, '94.
Silvanus Hemenway, 1770, '71, '72, '79, '80, '89, '90, '91.
Jonas Allen, 1770, '76, '77, '78, '80.
Benjamin Waite, 1774, '75, '76, '80.

Francis Chase, 1779, '81 '87, '88, '89.
Pelatiah Metcalf, 1779, '82, '86, '88, '90, '91.
Moulton Bullock, 1780, '81.
James Work, 1781.
John Orsborn. 1782, '86, '87, '92.
Jonas Thompson, 1782. Nathaniel Bragg, 1782,
John Bacheller, 1783, '90, '92, '93.
Jacob Esty. 1783, '84, '85, '86, '92, '94.
Henry Bond, 1783, '84, '85. Silas Heywood, 1783, '92.
Oliver Work, 1784, '85, '88, '89 '90. John Peck, 1787.
Samuel Goddard, 1791, 1801, 1802.
Isaac Gregory, 1792, '93, '95, '96, '97, '99, 1800, '06.
Shubel Blanding, 1793, '94. Nathan Bullock, 1795.
Ebenezer Fry, 1793, '94, '95, '96, '97, '98, '99, '1805, '06, '08.
John Norton from 1793 to 1803 inclusive, and from 1809 to 1817,
    excepting 1812.
Daniel Woodbury, 1795, '96 '98, '99, '1800, '14, '18, '19, '20.
James Forbes, 1796, '97. John Stockwell, 1797.
Ammi Falkner, 1798. Ebenezer Blanding, 1800.
Squier Davis, from 1800 to 1803, and from 1810 to 1826, inclusive,
    and 1829.
Joseph Estabrook, 1803, '04, '05, '08, '09, '10, '16.
Joseph Jacobs, 1804, '05, '06. Stephen Bacheller, Jr., 1807, '10.
Levi Thurston, 1807. Amos Jones, Jr., 1807, 1814.
Jonathan Gale, 1808, '09, '10. Rufus Bullock, 1811, '12, '13.
Thomas Richardson, 1812. John Holman, 1814, '18, '19, '20.
David Fisher, 1815. Nathan B. Newton, 1817.
Asahel Davis, 1817. '27, '28, '31, '32, '33.
Asa Bacheller, 1817, '21, '22 '23. William Pierce, 1821.
Benjamin Brown, 1821, '22, '23, '29, '30, '36.
Silas Jones, 1824, '25, '26, '27. '28, '31, '32, '33, '34, '35, '38, '39.
Russel Morse, 1824, '25 '26, '27, '28 '37 '38, '39, '40.
Stephen Richardson, 1829, '30, '46. Salmon Goddard, 1830.
Robert Thompson, 1831, '32, '33, '84, '36.
Joseph Davis, 2d, 1834, '35. Joseph Stockwell, 1835.
Benoni Peck, 1836, '37, '38, '39, '40, '43.
Arba Sherwin, 1837. Burnet Bullock, 1840. '44, '45.

Elmer Newton, 1841, Ebenezer Pierce, 1841, '42.
Hiram W. Albee, 1841, '42, '47, '48.   Daniel Bliss, 1844.
Benjamin Fry, 1842, '43, '51, '52.   Cyrus Davis, 1845.
Otis Gale, 1843, '44, '45, '46, '58.   Adriel White, 1846, '55.
Joseph Raymond, 1847, '48, '49 '50, '53, '54, '57, '58.
Jarvis Davis, 1847, '48 '50, '51, '54.   Tarrant Cutler, 1849.
Solyman Heywood, 1849.   Jesse F. Wheeler, 1850, 1851.
Otis Bemis, 1852, '53.   Nahum Longley, 1854, '59, '60.
Isaac Nichols, 1855.   Lemuel Fales, 1855, '56.
Cyrus B. Reed, 1856, '61, '62.   George Whitney, 1856.
L. W. Partridge, 1857.   Harvey W. Bliss, 1857.
Caleb A. Cook, 1858, '59, '60.   Richard Baker, 1861, '62.
Wm. W. Clement, from 1859, to 1865, inclusive.
J. A. Rich, 1863, '64, '65.   Hiram Harrington, 1863, '64, '65.

ASSESSORS WHEN A DIFFERENT BOARD FROM THE SELECTMEN.

John Fry, 1766, '78.   Wm. Town, 1766, '76, '77, '80.
Jonas Allen, 1766.   Henry Bond, 1773, '78, 81, '84, 85.
Benjamin Wait, 1773.   Stephen Bacheller, 1773.
Peter Woodbury, 1775, '76, '94.   David Lyon, 1775.
John Peck, 1775, '76, '80.   David Copeland, 1777.
Wm. Clement, 1777, 82.   Peletiah Metcalf, 1778, '94.
Timothy Bliss, 1779.   John Bacheller, 1779, '80.
Isaac Gale, 1779.   Oliver Work, 1781, '82, '83, '84, '85, '91.
Ebenezer Blanding, 1781, 1803, '04.   Samuel Goddard, 1783.
Joseph Emerson, 1782, '90, '94.   Jacob Esty, 1784, '85.
Ammi Falkner, 1783, '86, '87, '88, '89, '91, '92, '93 '97, '98
    1800, '02, '03, '04, '05, '06, 1807, '08 '09, '10.
Paul Ellis, 1786, '87, '88, '89, '90, '91, '93, '95, '96, '97, '98.
Daniel Woodbury, 1786, '87, '99, 1814, '15, '16, '20.
Isaac Gregory, 1788, '89, '90, '92, '93, '95 '98, '99, 1800, '02,
    '03, '05.
Eliphalet Cheney, 1795, '96.   John Norton, 1799, 1801.
David Fisher, 1796, '97, 1813, '14, '15, '16, '17.
Salmon Goddard, 1800, '01, '02, '05, '06, '10, '37.
Amos Jones, Jr. 1804, '06, '07, '08, '09, '13, '14.

Rufus Bullock, 1807, '13, '21, '22, '25, '26.
Isaac Metcalf, 1808, '09, '10.   Silas Heywood, 1817.
Tarrant Cutler, 1815, '16, '17, '21, '22, '23, '24, '27, '28, '29.
Benoni Peck, 1819, '20, '27, '30, '36, '40.
Silas Jones, 1819, '20, '30, '31, '32, '33 '34, '35, '36.
Asahel Davis, 1821, '22, '23, '24, '25 '26 '28, '29, '31, '32, '33.
Jonathan Peirce, 1823, '24, '27, 28, '29, 31.
Benjamin Brown, 1825.   Stephen Richardson. 1826.
Jonathan Gale, 1830.   Joseph Davis, 2d, '34 '35.
Russel Morse, 1832, '33, 34, '35, '36, 37, '40.
Arba Sherwin, 1827, '41.   Joseph Estabrook, 1840, '41.
Jarvis Davis, 1841, '50, '55.   Peter Woodbury, 1842.
Tarrant Cutler, 1842, '44, '45.   Luther Harrington, 1841.
Adriel White, 1842, '44, '45, '46.   George Peirce, 1844, '45, 46, 50.
Otis Gale, 1850.   Franklin Richardson, 1855.
Lemuel Fales, 1855.   Joseph Raymond, 1857, '58.
L. W. Patridge, 1857,   Henry W. Bliss, 1857, '58.
Jesse W. Wheeler, 1858.   Solymon Heywood, 1860.
Nahum Longley, 1860.   Joseph L. Perkins, 1860.

SUPPLEMENTARY NOTE.

Mr. Henry Peck, of Winchendon, has lately erected an appropriate marble slab at the grave of Nahum Green. Special credit is due to Mr. Horace Peirce, who has taken this matter in hand, and, aided by the subscriptions of several gentlemen of town, and the liberal discount of Mr. Peck, has now the satisfaction of seeing the work completed.

In Illustrating *Ezekiel Cutler*, (page 93) a generation was dropped. He was succeeded by his S., Ebenezer, who m. Phebe Wyman in 1785; raised up a family; settled his S., Ezekiel, with him; and finally removed from town with him. His S., Ezekiel, had one, or more children born to him here. Rev. Ebenezer Cutler, of Worcester, one of the family, was born here.

Dea. Benj. Woodbury, (page 93,) was succeeded by his S., Capt. Lot, who m. Martha Waite in 1778; and whose children were born, and some of them settled in town.

Silvanus Hemenway, (page 103,) should have been located, we now are inclined to believe, on the site occupied by the farm-house and buildings of Barnet Bullock Esq.—This surname, in the records, is spelled as above.

Jonathan Cutler, (page 104) is probably located wrong. Our present information would assign his original settlement just west of the corner of the roads between Col. Elmer Newton and Col. Benj. Brown's. Nathan B. Newton bought of him; and the present proprietor remembers to have assisted in filling up the old cellar-hole of the original dwelling house, on the site above indicated.

	PAGE.
Preface,	3
Report of Centennial,	5
Address, by His Excellency, Alex. H. Bullock,	21
Poem, by Rev. Albert Bryant,	68
Our Birthday,	79
Titles, Territory, and Proprietors,	79
Scenery,	84
Act of Outlawry,	87
Proprietors' Records,	88
Our Charter,	90
Early Settlers,	92
Religious Societies,	138
Hon. Rufus Bullock,	139
Wild Beasts and Game,	143
Roads,	147
The Doctors Bacheller,	150
Revolutionary Period, and Soldiers,	152
Last War with Great Britian, and Soldiers,	161
The War with the Rebellion, and Soldiers,	165
Education,	171
Graduates,	177
Longevity,	178
Industrial Pursuits,	180
Burial Grounds,	186
Robbing the Grave-Yard,	189
Elizabeth Lady Temple,	191
Public Gatherings,	192
Warnang out of Town,	195
Persecution of the Birds,	196
Obsolete Town Officers,	197
The Bleeders,	199
Delegates, Senators, Representatives, and Town Officers,	200
Supplementary Note,	206

www.ingramcontent.com/pod-product-compliance
Lightning Source LLC
Chambersburg PA
CBHW031814220426
43662CB00007B/642